CITY (IF APPLICABLE)

AGENCY

IN THE COURT DESIGNATED BELOW THE UNDERSIGNED CERTI... JUST AND REASONABLE GROUNDS TO BELIEVE AND DOES BE...

DAY OF WEEK SAT | MONTH 10 | A.M. | P.M.

NAME (PRINT) FIRST William | MIDDLE David | LAST Lane

STREET 4155 Dow Rd. | IF DIFFERENT THAN ONE ON DRIVER LICENSE "X" HERE

CITY | STATE FL | ZIP CODE 32934

TELEPHONE NUMBER | DATE OF BIRTH MO | DAY | YR | RACE W | SEX M | HGT

DRIVER LICENSE NUMBER | STATE | CLASS | CDL LICENSE | YR LICENSE EXP. | IF COMMERCIAL MTR. VEH. "X" HERE

PAY FINE OR REQUEST COURT DATE IN WRITING VOLUSIA COUNTY CLERK P.O. BOX 6043 DAYTONA BEACH FL 32122

YR. VEHICLE 1945 | MAKE | STYLE | COLOR | IF PLACARDED HAZARDOUS MATERIAL "X" HERE

VEHICLE LICENSE NO. | TRAILER TAG NO. | STATE FL | YEAR TAG EXPIRES 2001 | IF COMPANION CITATION(S) "X" HERE

UPON A PUBLIC STREET OR HIGHWAY, OR OTHER LOCATION, NAMELY

I-95 NB 1 Mi. South of LPGA Blvd.

FT. ____ MILES ____ N S E W OF NODE ____

DID UNLAWFULLY COMMIT THE FOLLOWING OFFENSE. CHECK ONLY ONE OFFENSE EACH CITATION.

- UNLAWFUL SPEED ____ MPH SPEED APPLICABLE ____ MPH
- (INTERSTATE 4-LANE HWY WITH 20 FT. MEDIAN OUTSIDE BUS. OR RES. DIST.)
- CARELESS DRIVING
- SAFETY BELT VIOLATION
- EXPIRED DRIVER LICENSE
- VIOLATION OF TRAFFIC CONTROL DEVICE
- IMPROPER OR UNSAFE EQUIPMENT
- FOUR (4) MONTHS OR LESS

A 054539

...arning
...hway Patrol

TIME 2142

HEIGHT | SEX

WEIGHT

...ATE | DOB

STATE

...SE NO. | STATE

...SE NO. | STATE

...ns Of STATE LAW

- Head Light
- Tail Light
- Stop Light
- Signal Light
- Windshield
- Tires/Wheels
- Exhaust
- License Plate
- Size/Weight
- Log Book
- Dangling Objec...
- Insurance

FLORIDA UNIFORM TRAFFIC CITATION 640497-M CHECK DIGIT X

COUNTY OF Volusia | (1) F.H.P. | (2) P.D. | (3) S.O. | (4) OTHER

CITY (IF APPLICABLE) | AGENCY Volusia County

IN THE COURT DESIGNATED BELOW THE UNDERSIGNED CERTIFIES THAT HE/SHE HAS JUST AND REASONABLE GROUNDS TO BELIEVE AND DOES BELIEVE THAT ON

SUMMONS (DEFENDANT'S COPY)

DAY OF WEEK SAT | MONTH 03 | DAY 11 | YEAR 2000 | 745 | A.M. | P.M.

NAME (PRINT) FIRST William | MIDDLE David | LAST

STREET 4155 Dow Rd. Apt. | IF DIFFERENT THAN ONE ON DRIVER LICENSE "X" HERE

CITY Melbourne | STATE FL | ZIP CODE

TELEPHONE NUMBER | DATE OF BIRTH MO | DAY 06 | YR | RACE | SEX | HGT

DRIVER LICENSE NUMBER | STATE FL | CLASS | YR. LICENSE EXP. | IF COMMERCIAL MTR. VEH. "X" HERE

YR. VEHICLE 52 | MAKE Harley | STYLE | COLOR Black | IF PLACARDED HAZARDOUS MATERIAL "X" HERE

VEHICLE LICENSE NO. FATCHOP | STATE FL | YEAR TAG EXPIRES 2001 | IF COMPANION CITATION(S) "X" HERE

UPON A PUBLIC STREET OR HIGHWAY, OR OTHER LOCATION, NAMELY

U.S. 1 @ Lowndes

FT. ____ MILES ____ N S E W OF NODE ____

DID UNLAWFULLY COMMIT THE FOLLOWING OFFENSE. CHECK ONLY ONE OFFENSE EACH TICKET.

- UNLAWFUL SPEED ____ MPH. SPEED APPLICABLE ____ MPH
- (INTERSTATE 4-LANE HWY. WITH 20 FT. MEDIAN OUTSIDE BUS. OR RES. DIST.)
- CARELESS DRIVING
- SAFETY BELT VIOLATION
- EXPIRED DRIVER LICENSE
- VIOLATION OF TRAFFIC CONTROL DEVICE
- IMPROPER OR UNSAFE EQUIPMENT
- FOUR (4) MONTHS OR LESS
- VIOLATION OF RIGHT-OF-WAY
- EXPIRED TAG
- MORE THAN FOUR (4) MONTHS
- IMPROPER CHANGE OF LANE OR COURSE
- FOUR (4) MONTHS OR LESS
- NO VALID DRIVER LICENSE
- IMPROPER PASSING
- MORE THAN FOUR (4) MONTHS
- DRIVING WHILE LICENSE SUSPENDED OR REVOKED
- CHILD RESTRAINT
- NO PROOF OF INSURANCE
- DRIVING UNDER THE INFLUENCE OF ALCOHOLIC BEVERAGES, CHEMICAL OR CONTROLLED SUBSTANCES; DRIVING/ACTUAL PHYSICAL CONTROL WHILE IMPAIRED, OR DRIVING/ACTUAL PHYSICAL CONTROL WITH UNLAWFUL BLOOD ALCOHOL LEVEL OF .10 PERCENT OR ABOVE.

BLOOD ALCOHOL LEVEL ____ %.

OTHER VIOLATIONS OR COMMENTS PERTAINING TO OFFENSE:

No front brake

IN VIOLATION OF: LOCAL ORDINANCE | STATE STATUTE | SECTION 316.610 | SUB-SECTION

CRASH YES NO | PROPERTY DAMAGE YES $ ____ NO | INJURY TO ANOTHER YES NO | SERIOUS BODILY INJURY TO ANOTHER YES NO | FATAL YES NO

- CRIMINAL VIOLATION, COURT APPEARANCE REQUIRED, AS INDICATED BELOW.
- INFRACTION, COURT APPEARANCE REQUIRED, AS INDICATED BELOW.
- INFRACTION WHICH DOES NOT REQUIRE APPEARANCE IN COURT

640497-M CHECK DIGIT X

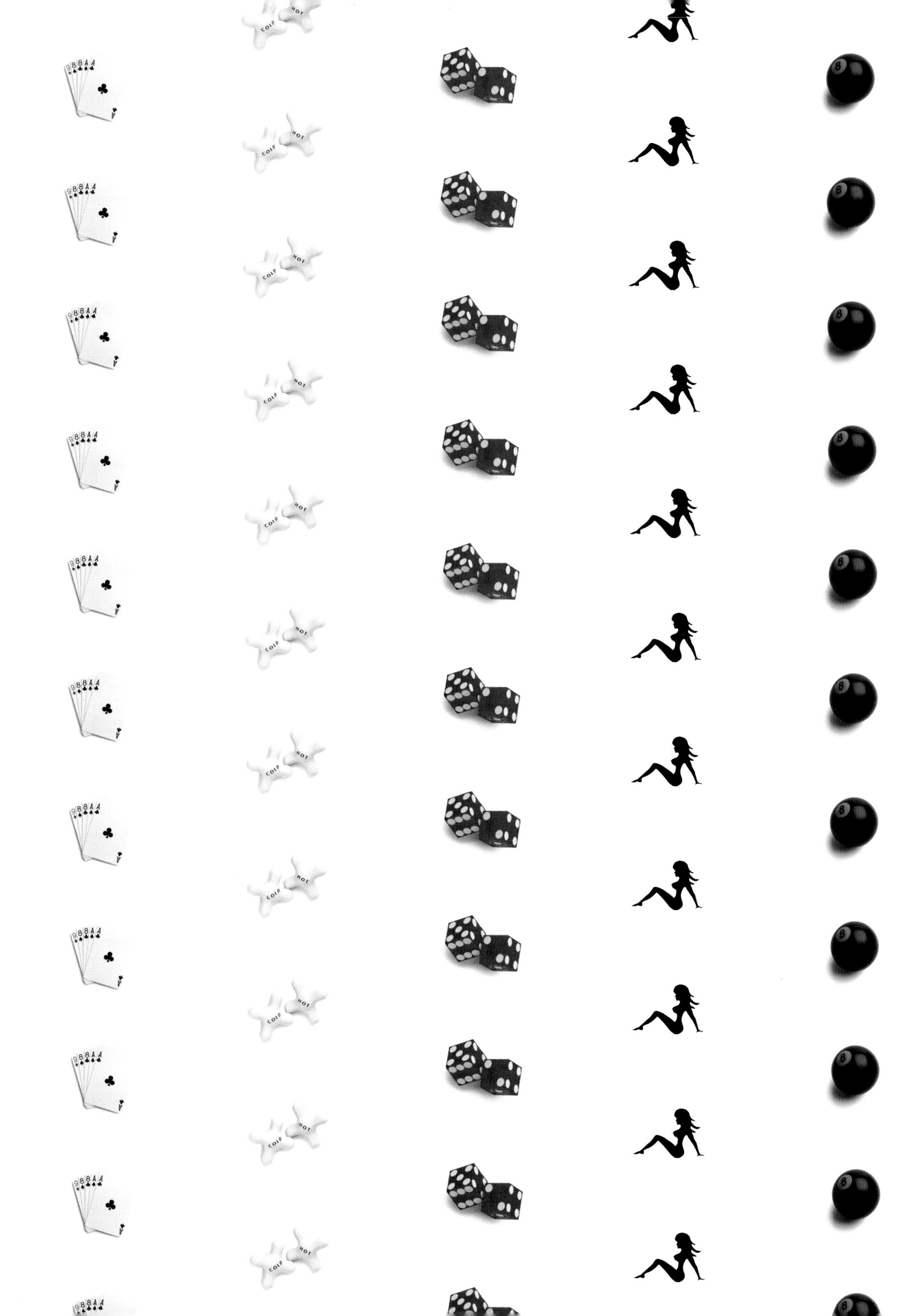

BILLY LANE

PHOTOGRAPHY BY
MICHAEL LICHTER

BILLY LANE

CHOP FICTION

WITH
DARWIN HOLMSTROM

It's NOT a motorcycle baby, it's a Chopper!

MOTORBOOKS
INTERNATIONAL

Author Photo

This edition first published in 2004 by Motorbooks International, an imprint of MBI Publishing Company, Galtier Plaza, Suite 200, 380 Jackson Street, St. Paul, MN 55101-3885 USA

ISBN: 0-7603-2011-X

Edited by Zack Miller and Darwin Holmstrom
Designed by Rochelle Schultz

Printed in China

Foreword

AFTER OBSERVING a final product—whether it's a car, a piece of art, an interior design, or a piece of architecture—you either end up liking it or not, without thinking about the person behind the design. When it comes to motorcycles, the creativity, engineering, craftsmanship, and details tell us much about the person behind the machine. Billy Lane creates kustom machines and a kustom creation is what makes up Billy Lane.

The way he expresses his personality through his machines singles Billy out from other bikers and bike builders.

The attitude and fun that characterize his personality are present in the workmanship on his unique bikes. Along with the enjoyment he finds in his work, he enjoys the company of the enthusiasts he did that work for!

So, Billy, keep those two wheels easy riding. That's you, Billy Lane; you're just a cool guy.

—George Barris
May 2004

With George, 2004

George Barris Collection

Photographer's Notes: The Artist Comes to Light

By Michael Lichter

IT WAS MY JOB—if traveling around America just to shoot the best custom Harleys in America can be considered a job. That's why I was in Charlotte, South Carolina, at the Easyriders Bike Show in January 2000. Each of the top-six winning bikes at the show had to be photographed in my traveling studio for a full bike feature in *Easyriders* magazine. This may not seem like a lot of bikes to shoot, but each motorcycle was photographed on a studio background from six different angles with as many as one-hundred details and overall shots. I knew I would be shooting all day Saturday during the show, past midnight when the public was cleared out, and possibly right until the sun came up Sunday morning.

Food was brought in so I could keep shooting uninterrupted. It was like a marathon, but somehow I found time to take a quick walk through the show to get a feel for the bikes, like I try to do at all the shows. Each venue has a different look. At that time, I connected Charlotte with full-bodied bikes that had lots of graphics, the occasional theme bike, and a smattering of perfectly restored antiques.

In the midst of probably 150 amazing show bikes sat a simple shovelhead chopper with dual carbs called "Money Magnet" that got my attention. It had a long front end, peanut tank, blue paint job with a pin-up graphic, and great lines. The bike didn't look like it would be getting one of the top-six trophies to insure a spot in my studio, but I wanted to photograph it anyway and asked my editor what he thought. He was concerned that I couldn't get that many feature bikes shot at a show but I insisted I could do it. And I did. I believe my assistant Steve Temple and I left the venue with the studio packed and seven bikes shot before 6 a.m. I even made a portrait of the builder sitting on the bike. He posed looking very self-confident wearing a pair of slacks and a pork pie hat. While I had never heard of this builder before, his bike, his look, and his entourage all intrigued me. He was "arty" and his style different. This was my introduction to Billy Lane.

The following year, while making arrangements to shoot the Charlotte show again, I got in touch with Billy. He told me about some new bikes, Devil-in-a-Red-Dress and Blue Death Trap, that he would have at the show, so I got the OK from Easyriders to set up a day early to shoot them. The extra day allowed me more time to meet his friends. George was there since Death Trap was his, along with Nick, Daisy, Billy's girlfriend Claudia, and a few others. It was a great group of people all bound together by Billy, his talent, and his bikes.

After Charlotte, 2001, I stayed in closer touch with Billy. He had a unique kind of energy and creativity that I hadn't seen before. I began to see him as an artist, mixing engineering and metal fabrication skills with found art in the medium of motorcycles.

That summer I asked him to put a bike in an exhibition I was organizing at the Journey Museum in Rapid City, South Dakota, which was scheduled to coincide with Sturgis that August. He would be the young blood I would display next to the work of customizing legends Arlen Ness, Donnie Smith, Eddie Trotta, and Ron Simms, as well as younger stars like Paul Yaffe and Jesse James. Knuckle Sandwich lived up to all my expectations when it arrived in my Sturgis studio to be photographed just prior to the exhibition opening. He also brought a new Panhead called "Pimp Daddy" for me to shoot. This brought the number of his bikes that were shot for Easyriders to five in just 18 months. Billy was

On Money Magnet, from Michael Lichter's very first photo shoot of one of my bikes.

On Knuckle Sandwich, 2001.

getting on the map quickly. Each bike seemed to be a new exploration. Billy was getting quirkier and I liked it.

That same year at Sturgis I had my first opportunity to photograph another side of Billy—him out riding with friends. He left the Buffalo Chip where he was camping in the dust and mud (and having a great time) to head north past Bear Butte into that beautiful western landscape. How different the landscape from south Florida, but Billy fit perfectly as he rode Devil through the Dakota plains with Claudia on the back. George was with us riding Billy's Panhead SweetMaryJane, which George had crashed in the campground the night before. He got into my face (and lens) with his signature quick gestures. It was simple and fun, friends out for a ride.

I saw Billy a few months later in Daytona Beach during Biketoberfest. He was previewing a "roller" in his Choppers Inc. booth that wasn't near finished. It was an amazing bike with a hubless rear wheel. I had heard of this idea but had never seen one before and wondered if he could really finish it and if it would really work. He promised me he would have it ready to shoot in Columbus, Ohio, four months later. The "engineering Billy" came on strong that winter to get the bike to ride properly, but before he appeared in Columbus with the finished bike, the "artist Billy" finessed it. His ability to tie art and science together with a unique style began to shine with this bike.

It takes a few hours to shoot each bike feature. Much of the time is spent on my stomach, looking up at a bike in that monumental perspective to discover details that many people never notice. PsychoBilly Cadillac had even more elements for me to discover and work with than Billy's other bikes.

The best bikes from across the nation were at this show, but everyone knew this bike was special. Spectators stared in disbelief. Billy took the Best of Show trophy at this, the final and biggest invitational show of the winter season. From that moment on, Billy would be seen in a different light. The year 2002 was to be one of change, growth, and recognition. Life was speeding up for Billy.

Through this same period, the motorcycle world was changing drastically. The Camel Roadhouse motorcycle tour had been putting a few select builders on a pedestal for several years, then the Discovery Channel raised the bar higher when they followed one of these builders, Jesse James, to Sturgis to make *Motorcycle Mania,* a one-hour special in 2000. No one could have foreseen the spectacular success this show would achieve. It repeated over and over and was quickly followed with a sequel. The motorcycle "superstar" was born and he was Jesse. Crowds would form around him as he was asked to autograph everything from t-shirts to women's body parts. Licensees and rock stars sought him out. *Monster Garage,* the cable television show, was created around Jesse to bring his look and attitude into the average American household as entertainment. Who could have predicted that motorcycles could change the cable TV industry? This really was to be a new millennium.

Jesse helped bring attention to many friends by inviting them to appear on *Monster Garage* as guests. Billy was right there when they started filming, which provided his entrée to Discovery. Plans were put into motion, and from May through June they filmed the first *Biker Build-Off* between Billy and Roger Bourget. They rode to *The Horse* magazine's Smokeout as the cameras rolled. Bikers at the Smokeout picked Billy's MissBehavin' to win the build-off and with this new title under his belt, he rode from the Smokeout to Sturgis.

Arriving in South Dakota with his back tire missing a lot of tread and still fresh with road grime, Billy pulled the bike into my Sturgis

Michael took this photo without knowing who I was. We wouldn't meet for another year and a half.

studio on Tuesday night of bike week. I knew we had to shoot it before riding off the next morning on Wyoming Wednesday. Good thing, because by the end of the day Wednesday, after riding hard all day with Niki on back, he pulled it into the Sundance, Wyoming, burnout pit and "smoked it till the wheels fell off." I took the photo titled "That's Why We're Here" just before the tire popped. After commenting how awesome the burnout was, I asked him how he would get back to Sturgis almost one hundred miles away. He truly had not thought about it. This was a shot I missed: Billy riding my Road King with a windshield all the way back, his first and only time on a "bagger." (Steve came out and picked up me and Missbehavin' with our truck.)

The next two years flew by with new bikes appearing at a quicker pace as Billy achieved more and more notoriety. The first Discovery Channel *Biker Build-Off* was followed by a second against Dave Perewitz and a third against Indian Larry. He was invited to join the Camel Roadhouse Tour in 2003 and then the Easyriders Centerfold Tour and the ChopShop Tour in 2004. Despite traveling somewhere almost every weekend, he has managed to keep turning out fresh and innovative bikes. Not limited to any one style, he keeps working in different directions. While his very complex Camel hubless bike took that concept to a new height, he has also explored simpler styles like his Hell'sBelle bobber that looks back to the roots of custom motorcycles. Not everyone gets what Billy is doing and that is perfectly OK with him. On a ride from Florida to Texas, a journalist came up to me and, referring to the Discovery Channel Build-Off bike Agent Orange, asked what I thought—because he didn't get it either. I knew he had a music background, so I asked him how he liked his kid's music. After answering that he didn't like it, I commented, "That's it!" Agent Orange is just something different, a new way of looking at the same old thing.

I have continued to meet up with Billy around the country, visit his shop, ride with him, have him visit me at my home, and photograph his bikes for *Easyriders* Magazine. He is much busier now but he still makes time to meet up with old friends like Bean're, Billy, Chuck, and Booster and, on a recent ride to Vegas, motorcycling inspirations like Mondo and Ron Finch. They have always supported him, and now there are so many fans. Billy seems to always be recognized. At the curbside check-in at Denver airport the attendant said, "I know who you are, I don't need no ID from you." Despite the long lines that form at events just to shake his hand, he seems to make time for each person. He'll autograph anything they put in front of him (paper or flesh), pose with them for photos, and ask them about their bikes. He has become an inspiration to countless bikers who have their own quirky ideas about what they want to roll down the highway on and for whom Billy represents the ultimate biker success.

I have known Billy less than five years, but in that time I have seen him push himself and grow to new heights. As I wrote earlier, I knew he was "arty" but in the past few years he has certainly earned the title "artist" in my book.

Getting ready to take Helle'sBelle for its first ride.

AAA

INTRODUCTION

Skipping School

On Helle'sBelle in New Mexico, 2004.

AS I TYPE THIS, I am on a plane from California to Philly. I just finished filming a television show for the Discovery Channel called *Big.* I am on my way to a Harley-Davidson Dealership's annual customer appreciation party in Camden County, New Jersey. I never thought, as a kid building choppers on a concrete-block bench in my father's garage, that I'd be traveling coast-to-coast from a film set to a biker party. But, these days, that's as much a part of what I do for a living as is building custom motorcycles.

When I hear cliché expressions like "live your dreams," I have to wonder what living my dreams would've actually been like. I constantly hear people tell me how I have the "dream job" or the "dream life." Truth is, I never dreamed I'd be doing what I do for a living—or living the life that I live. I never aspired to be a custom bike builder, or to even make my living in the motorcycle industry. I began playing the guitar in the third grade, and I wanted to be a rock star. Cars, girls, and choppers came between me and my dreams. I began working on motorcycles out of

Riding with Nikki in South Dakota

necessity, because that's what bikers do. I worked on my own bike, and helped my friends out with theirs. At some unknown point, I realized I had to make decision about what I was going to do with my life. I chose to make motorcycles my life, and to cast aside every other ambition I'd ever held. Which is why I can write what I write on these pages with a clear conscience and without apology. Not many people can do that truthfully.

There is much that I would like to write that I simply cannot write in this book, and many people suggested I probably shouldn't have written much of what I did. I do my own thing, but putting some of those things in print is dangerous business. I'm opinionated about

On the bike we built for the VQ auction, 2003. That's Kim Suter beside me.

When you get to ride a chopper into the winner's circle at Daytona as part of your job, you must be doing something right.

choppers and the people whose lives connect with them, because I'm passionate and protective of the lifestyle choppers have afforded me. There are people and events I have purposely left out, for my own selfish reasons. I will allude to some of the omissions, and many people who know me will understand what I mean. For those of you who don't, ask me in person. I'm always on the road, and I will be candid with you.

Many of the names that I have mentioned have inspired, influenced, and driven me, and I hope to touch a few readers in the very same way. In many ways my work is my interpretation of their work. Were it not for the people who created and kept the aftermarket Harley industry and custom bike world alive through lean times, I wouldn't be writing these words. As much as this is about myself, my life, my bikes, my friends, and my business, it is a tribute to the people who are responsible for making me want to be who I am. Every sleepless night, every broken heart, every dirty deed has been worth it to me to be where I am today.

It is humbling to reflect on and put in print the last sixteen years of my life in the short period of seven months that it has taken to write this book. Conversations with people, photographs, and personal articles I have found have ignited memories that would have been all but forgotten. As we all do, I have to live with the consequences of my actions and my words. So many people have asked me for my story that I think writing this book is a risk I have to take.

4BM

chapter ONE

The Streets of Miami

My brother, Warren with me at Sturgis in 1998.

Author Photo

I'VE LIVED all of my life in Florida. I grew up in Miami, where my dad was one of the crew schedulers and my mother was a flight attendant for National Airlines. This was back in the day when airline pilots were more like rock stars. The pilots smoked, drank, and made more money than they do today. They had to do a lot more to earn that money, though. Everything wasn't computerized—they used to land the airplanes themselves.

My dad worked directly with the flight attendants in a time when most were female and we called them stewardesses. They all knew him and they frequently needed favors from him. The schedulers for the pilots shared the same offices, so dad knew them all well. This was back when stewardesses were hired for their looks. They had to be young and hot, and meet unfair weight and appearance restrictions. This was in the 1960s through the early 1980s, and life was different. A lot of things went on in airplanes that don't go on today.

The pilots and stewardesses would give my dad gifts to make sure certain other pilots and stewardesses would be on the same flights they were on. It was like a big dating service with airplanes and luggage. The pilots would give my dad gifts like clothes, Miami Dolphins tickets, and I'm sure all kinds of crazy shit that I haven't been told about.

That's how my parents met. Mom was young and hot, and she was the one who got Dad to settle down and raise a family when his options with women were open and huge. She is a smart woman so she had to know what was going on. She had to know what my dad was up to before he met her. He is thirteen years older than her, and she was only nineteen when they met. It was a pretty radical move for her, and tricky I bet.

My parents, Warren and Marion Lane at the shop in 2003.

My dad quit working for the airline when I was a teenager. The airlines had a lot of management problems, and the labor unions were always at odds with the management. The employees would go on strike, and the family would be at home with no paycheck. Crossing a picket line of striking union workers was not my dad's style, so he had to find another source of income. Dad was always a gearhead and he restored old MGs as a hobby. He made money from his hobby and supported our family with it. One day my older brother Warren brought home an old Corvette that he'd bought from one of our neighborhood drug dealers. It was really beat up, full of bullet holes. He fixed it up, and that project started our family restoring old Corvettes. Corvettes were the shit in Miami back then and the Corvette market was really strong. Eventually my dad took advantage of the opportunity to quit working for the airline, and began restoring Corvettes for a living.

I always worked as a kid. Mike Plymyl, one of my parents' flight attendant friends, owned a landscaping company, and when I was thirteen years old I started working for him on weekends and during school vacations. Mike gave me my first job at M&D Property Services. He expected me to work hard, but his personality was colorful as hell and working for him was entertaining. He looked out for me, and reinforced the values and manners my parents laid on me. Mike cussed with every sentence, and I think I'm going to blame my habit of doing the same on him.

I worked for M&D for a couple of years, until another flight attendant (who was also one of my mother's closest friends) asked her husband to hire me. I got a job at East Coast Tank Sealing, which repaired fuel tank leaks and damage on large jet aircraft at Miami International Airport. My boss' name was Don Bowers, and he was even

Just starting the gas tank on my Chop Shop tour bike.

My parents taught me that if you want something, you have to work hard to get it.

The magazine *Easyriders* played a big role in my becoming interested in choppers.

more colorful than Mike was. Don was probably already into his sixties when I worked for him, but he had the fire and energy of a four year old. I was still in high school, and I would go out drinking with my friends Friday night—knowing I had to be at work the next morning at 7:00.

Don would berate me for it, but he had my best interests at heart. He worked hard and took his profession very seriously. Even more so than with motorcycles, safety is a predominant issue when working with aircraft. Don stressed safety with every opportunity. I constantly find myself doing the same thing at Choppers, Inc. When something gets done in a rushed or sloppy manner, it drives me crazy.

Don and his crew foreman, Terry, kept me on my toes. They taught me how to think three steps ahead. That is one of the most valuable lessons I've learned, and I use it every day. Don paid very well for good, hard work. He was already a success, and I watched Terry—only in his mid-twenties at the time—succeed and enjoy life. I watched those guys build strong, productive lives and wanted to do the same. That job meant a lot to me, and I learned enormous life lessons from it.

I saved my money and bought a wrecked 1957 Chevy BelAir by the time I was 15. I helped my dad fix it, and he taught me how to drive in it. I sold it for a profit and bought a 1969

I credit much of my success to the way my parents raised me, to the values they instilled in me, and I still appreciate their advice and support.

convertible Camaro Indianapolis 500 Pace Car, which I drove for about three months. I got a good offer on it and sold it to buy my first Corvette. It was a Nassau Orange 1972 Stingray, and I street raced it almost daily. I paid $4,500 for it, and someone saw it sitting in my folks' yard two weeks after I brought it home, and offered me $7,000 for it. I was quickly learning that wrenching could make me money. I bought a 1969 Stingray that needed some work after I sold the 1972, and we fixed it up. I couldn't afford to buy a pristine car so I bought one that needed work. My dad really liked the car, so I traded it to him for his 1966 Corvette coupe. I wrecked that car street racing my junior year in high school, nearly totaling it. My parents were pissed. The car was so nice that I was able to sell its mangled remains for $10,000. My next 'Vette was a 1972 that needed quite a bit of work. My dad and brother helped me with it, and we restored it, turning it into a very nice car. I owned that car throughout my sentence in college, hardly driving it at all. By then I was completely hooked on motorcycles.

Billy Lane, car freak.

I inherited my love of cars from my dad.

The female body influences all the bikes I design.

Choppers and the Female Body

WHEN I WAS A KID we used to go to the Tropicare Drive-In, this old drive-in movie theater that had been converted into a flea market. One day Warren bought a stack of old *Easyriders* magazines there. My mother didn't know what they were—she didn't know about the nudity. *Easyriders* used to show much more nudity in the 1970s and 1980s than it does today. Mom just thought they were motorcycle magazines.

She eventually figured out what they were and took them away, but until then I studied those magazines. Warren and I used to sleep out in a tent in our backyard and read the magazines with flashlights. Warren wouldn't really let me look at them. He liked to mess with me like that. But I'd sneak a look at them whenever I could. Those images are burned into me, the outlaws, the women, and the bikes. I used to wonder how those dirty long-haired dudes scored such beautiful women. Now I know. I was fascinated by it all, and still am.

To this day I associate choppers with the female body. I build them like a woman: curvy hips, thin waist, then widening out on top, something to hang on to while you're riding them. When it comes to choppers and women, I like mine wild and crazy, slender, and soft. In a time when everyone is building enormous, oversized, overdone bikes, I like my bike compact and my woman petite. If I'm going to ride it, it's got to be mine. I don't want anyone else's.

To me, the perfect ride is 800 pounds: 500 pounds of Milwaukee steel chopped with love just right, me, and a nice little 100-pounder on the back fender hanging on because she wants to.

I've always been a huge fan of Vargas-style pin-up art. This piece is by Gil Elvgren.

I build them like women...

...Curvy hips, thin waist, then widening out on top...

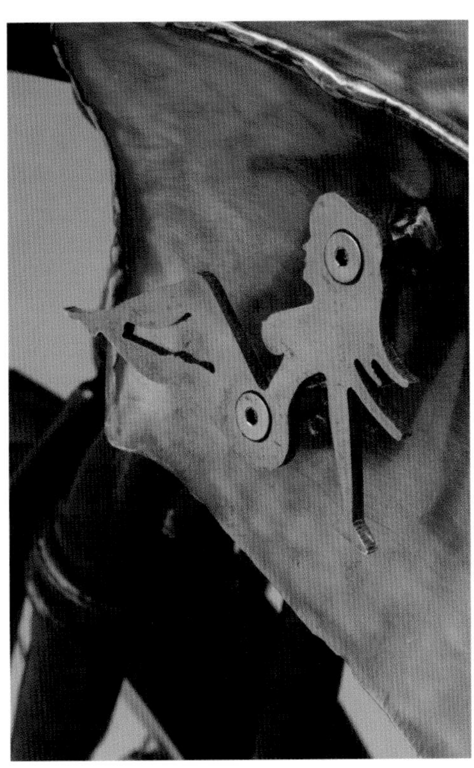

Painter Joe Richardson, with Chop Shop's gas tank.

...Something to hang on to while you're riding them...

My first Panhead and first Daytona Bike Week, 1989. No tattoos.

Author Photo

Busting My Chopper Cherry

FOR AS LONG AS I CAN REMEMBER, all I ever wanted to do was drink beer, surf, ride motorcycles, and raise hell with my friends. I'd been working on and restoring vintage Corvettes with my brother and father for a couple of years, throughout high school. Drinking beer, surfing, and raising hell were already in place, and motorcycles were soon to follow. This was the late 1980s, and the craze for Harley-Davidsons and the other American Big-Twin motorcycles to follow them had yet to really take off.

The scene was gaining momentum, though, and it was already pretty strong in Europe. South Beach itself was in its infancy in becoming the scene it is today, and it was a popular destination for European vacationers. Dad and Warren had already exported a couple of 'Vettes to Europe and had received many requests for older Harley-Davidsons to be sent overseas, especially choppers. Choppers became a part of the business, and a part of my life. I liked working on them because of their mechanical simplicity. Choppers were like the vintage 'Vettes: You had to work on them all day Saturday if you wanted to be able to ride one Saturday night. But they were worth every pull of the wrench and twist of the screwdriver, and that made the ride even more rewarding.

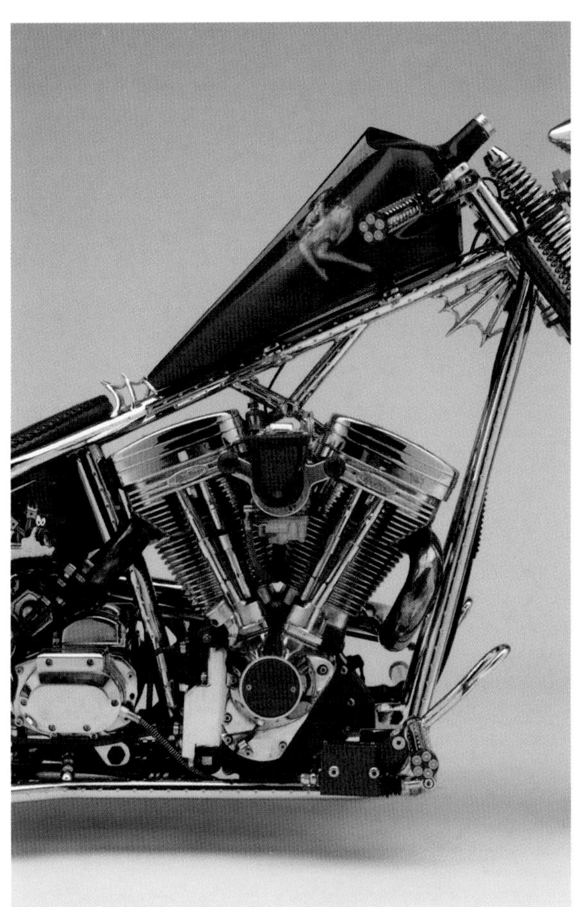

Even though choppers were a part of the family business, my parents still forbade either of us to have motorcycles. Warren, being the more rebellious child, finally broke through their anti-motorcycle blockade when he bought a 1979 Shovelhead chopper. Warren—in my dad's absence—encouraged me to ride the Shovelhead down First Street in Miami Beach one afternoon. First Street was located in what is called South Point, the triangular section of the beachside that existed south of Fifth Street between Florida's intracoastal waterway and the Atlantic Ocean. Today it's an exclusive neighborhood; I think they even spell Point with an "e" attached to the end now. But during my first chopper ride, it was a ghetto slum where the dealers, junkies, skaters, surfers, hookers, thieves, and losers existed in a sort of twisted harmony. And we were there, too. It was an experience I'll never forget.

If Mom had known how interested Warren and I were in motorcycles, she probably wouldn't have let us sit on this bike in 1975. *Author Photo*

I had ridden a few of my friends' sportbikes before, but this thing was entirely different. The foot pegs and controls were in front of my body, rather than behind it. The springer front fork was bouncy, and the front tire would un-weight with the slightest twist of the sensitive throttle, making it difficult to steer. The torque was unbelievable, and the 3-inch open primary belt drive was whining right next to my leg. I rode west down First Street, which curved north and became Alton Road north of Fifth Street. That curve was an alarming obstacle for me. The Chromoly Jim Davis rigid frame sent every bump of First Street right through the entire bike, and when the springer started to bounce and the steering slipped I squeezed the clutch instead of throttling, which would have settled the front end. I started to lose my balance and went straight through the curve, past the water tower—the most prominent landmark in the neighborhood at that time—with my feet down. Luckily, little traffic dared roll through South Point back then.

Warren's chopper had what we call the pancake-top-style four-speed transmission—a notoriously ambiguous device with which to row through the gears. I found it difficult to get the thing back into neutral, but I did, and turned the

Author Photo

bike around to head back toward the shop. Warren was too far away to hear over the gooseneck dragpipes, but I could see him laughing his ass off at me in the distance.

"Yeah, fuck you," I thought to myself. "I'm riding this thing." It all reminded me of my first sexual experience: Fear, confusion, thrill, and a sense of accomplishment. I remembered all of it a few years later when South Point(e) had become The Place To Be, and the City decided to tear down that water tower. All of the locals were upset to see the landmark torn down, each for his or her own reason. I had reasons of my own. I learned to surf there, rode my first chopper there, and made quite a few great, life-long friends down there. The water tower is gone, along with the fear and confusion I felt when I wobbled past it years ago; however the thrill and the sense of accomplishment that developed from that experience continue to drive and mystify me to this very day.

Me and Hannah, Devil's Tower, 2003.

To me, the perfect ride is 800 pounds: 500 pounds of Milwaukee steel chopped with love just right, me, and a nice little 100-pounder on the back fender.

If anything, Nick's even rowdier than I am.

Cocaine Cowboys

MY PARENTS were very conservative and even more strict about what they would allow us to do. Warren and I were expected to do well in school, exercise the manners we were taught, and be responsible for ourselves and our actions. We were expected to go to college and graduate. Miami was a pretty rough place to grow up in the 1980s and 1990s, and our parents didn't want us to become products of our environment.

We lived in a middle-class neighborhood, but the city was like the Wild West. Anyone who lived there during that time can tell you that the postcards of palm trees and coconuts on the beach didn't even come close to accurately depicting what was going on down there. Cuba opened its prisons and its borders, and the good and the bad made it across the Florida Straits. The good moved into South Florida and built businesses and new lives. The bad moved in and created newer and even better lives through crime. Right behind them were those who saw opportunity from all over the Caribbean, Central America, and South America.

Remains of Discovery's *Biker Build-Off 4* trophy.

Most of the time I have a lot of fun doing what I do.

SweetMaryJane, 1952 Panhead bobber.

Author Photo

The cocaine trade exploded, literally, onto the streets of Miami. Those involved most heavily were called the Cocaine Cowboys. Cocaine created a wealth and a lifestyle otherwise unobtainable for so many. It wasn't uncommon to have shootouts in traffic at intersections with fully automatic machine guns. The place was nuts. Hollywood and the press have been accused of exaggerating and sensationalizing things for the sake of entertainment, but films like *Scarface* and television shows like *Miami Vice* were pretty damn much on the mark in illustrating Miami in its wildest days. I don't think I know anyone from Miami whose life hasn't been tremendously impacted by what was happening back then. We grew up with crime all around us, and our parents did their best to keep us away from it.

I never tried cocaine, speed, or acid, even though it's always been all around me. I did ecstasy a couple of times and got dosed a third time. I liked it (except for the time I got dosed), but I'll never do it again. The second time I tried it is the reason I won't do it anymore. I was with my brother and my girlfriend. She asked if I had done ecstasy and I lied. I said I didn't, but she knew otherwise by the way I was acting. I felt so bad about lying to her that I never took ecstasy again. I don't like not being myself.

At the Full Throttle Saloon in Sturgis, 2003.

My fans come in all shapes and sizes.

Sometimes it gets a little out of hand. I'd be lying if I said I was a saint.

I'm pretty open-minded about drugs, but they're not really for me. I think people—adults—should be able to do whatever they want, as long as they are willing to live with the responsibility of their actions. I tried mushrooms a couple of times, once at a Gregg Allman concert. This was the time I got dosed. My buddy threw some ecstasy in my Jack on the rocks while I wasn't looking. Taking ecstasy and mushrooms at the same time—that shit will fuck you up good and proper. My girlfriend had to stand on top of me to hold me down. I was amping hard for a couple of hours, flashing from mellow and depressed to full-blown hallucinations. I'd done some wacky shit to my body, but this was over the top.

The second time I ate mushrooms was in Sturgis. I don't recommend that to anyone who plans to ride, but it sure made the riding interesting. My brain wasn't nearly as macked as it was during my first 'shroom experience, but Spearfish Canyon has never looked the same to me as it did that day. Weed doesn't bother me, and I think it should be legalized. In case you haven't heard, I like to drink beer, whiskey, and tequila more than most people you know. But I don't really have an addictive personality. I have it under control. When I want to go wild, I do. When I need to focus, I'm on time. I like a little balance. I was talking to my uncle the other day and we were discussing whether I was a workaholic. I told him not to worry, because I really don't want to work as much as I do. The only reason I work so hard now is because I don't want to work at all in 20 years. I want to be able to surf and ride my choppers.

Telling me I couldn't have a tattoo pretty much guaranteed I'd go out and get as many as I could fit on my body.

If I had become an engineer in the auto industry I don't think I'd be signing autographs on girl's breasts...

Higher Education

When I graduated high school, I was accepted to Florida State University in Tallahassee to pursue a degree in mechanical engineering. I was glad to leave Miami. I moved away, joined a fraternity, and mixed exorbitant amounts of booze with some studying thrown in for kicks. There was a bar right across the street from the frat house, which was a major attraction to me at first, and I'd be lying if I said that I didn't spend a significant amount of time there. I didn't do that well in school at first, mainly because I wasn't focused. I partied too much at the Chi Phi house.

But I was fortunate enough to have hard working parents with the concern and generosity to put me through college, and I felt obligated to remain in school and succeed. My grades improved, and I actually enjoyed studying. Strozier Library was full of hot chicks, and it added a social atmosphere to studying that kept me interested in school. *Playboy* magazine even chose Strozier as one of the top ten pick-up places in the nation.

...Or signing autographs on various other body parts.

Ironically, living at the frat house reinforced the lessons I learned from my folks, like the value of time management, financial responsibility, personal responsibility, respect, trust, integrity, and honesty. I loved the fraternity so much that I became involved in its leadership. Eventually I was elected president and lived the majority of my five years in Tallahassee in the fraternity house. Although I was originally attracted to the house because of the possibilities for partying 24 hours a day, by the time I left I had begun to focus on more serious things.

While in college, I waited tables for extra money and bought a 1979 Jeep CJ-5 with huge Mickey-Thompson tires, a full roll cage, and enough lights on it to bury the amperage gauge on the dashboard when I hit the switch. I had some fun with it, but I really had my eye on a 1977 Harley-Davidson Sportster that I saw when I was home visiting on Christmas break. My brother's friend Pete rode the Sporty all the way from California to Miami Beach. He arrived with virtually nothing else to his name but that motorcycle and needed to sell it for spending money. It was cool and black, with straight pipes and low drag handlebars. I wanted to buy it but my parents were totally against it. I begged and pleaded, and we fought about it for some time. I didn't understand why my brother was allowed to own a motorcycle and I wasn't.

Time to sign another autograph.

Warren had attended college in Miami but decided to abandon his education only a few credit hours short of earning a degree in business management. I was still in school, working, and had the money to pay the $2,000 price tag myself. I promised my parents that I'd graduate if they would only let me buy this thing. Their answer? A resounding "No!" And after seeing my fraternity brother (and childhood friend) Mike Crutchfield's fraternity tattoo, they added that if I came home with either a tattoo *or* a motorcycle that they would cease to pay for my education. I promised not to come home with either, but I had every intention to come home with both. I felt like my brother had always been favored by our folks, and that this was just another example.

My parents never thought I was serious about building choppers. They thought I was a responsible kid so they weren't too worried. I was still in college when I started building choppers. I was making money, and my parents assumed that when I finished school I'd go into the engineering field. I didn't give it much consideration back then. I figured I was just like most kids in their early twenties, waiting for opportunity to find me. About the time I was twenty-five, I became sick of waiting and sought out my future with some real diligence.

Chop Shop tour debut at Daytona, 2004.

I love to learn. That's what I got out of college—the ability to learn. I wasn't interested in engineering. For a while I transferred to fine arts, but I realized that if I stuck with engineering I'd learn how to learn. I considered the stuff they taught in the classroom nonsense, except for the fundamentals like mathematics and physics, but I learned how to think analytically in the engineering program. I ended up really liking college because of that. Well, that and Chi Phi.

When I was in school I thought I would become an engineer in the automotive industry, but that wasn't for me. I had originally wanted to be an automotive designer. That is on the art side of things, creating and styling the cars we drive. It's a lot more exciting now than it was in the early 1990s. Things happen a lot faster now due to advances in computer graphics, and engineers in the U.S. auto industry have a lot more creative freedom now than they did just a few years ago. I think I'd like working in the auto industry now, but then how many automotive engineers have beautiful women asking to have them sign their names on their breasts? I think I made the right choice.

Run down on my Panhead.

Author Photo

My First Chopper

EVEN THOUGH my parents had forbidden me to buy a motorcycle, I knew I was going to buy one. Warren said that if I bought a bike, I had to buy a chopper. That made sense to me.

I didn't buy Pete's Sporty, and I'm glad now. It wasn't a chopper. I sold my Jeep back at school and started looking for a bike. Warren told me to look for a Big Twin—one of the many times he gave me stand-up, solid advice. I looked all over Orlando, Tampa, St. Petersburg, and Jacksonville. Every weekend I went in search of what I'd been dreaming about for some time. Back then, I could have bought all of the 4-speed swingarm FLH's and Superglides in Florida for $4,500 each, cash money. Harley-Davidson had just released its Fat Boy model, and everyone wanted one. Old Shovels and Panheads were everywhere for low dollars.

Author Photo

In early 1989 I bought a 1950 Panhead in Marianna, Florida, for $2,700. That was, without question, the best money I'll ever spend. It was complete, but the guy I bought it from was generous enough to have dismantled it

If you like riding old Harleys, you've got to love working on them. *Author Photo*

completely for me. His name was Richard. I can't remember his last name. His wife wanted that bike gone more than I wanted it to be mine. I did good, selling my Jeep for $4,500. I had money left over for parts and beer and that's what I spent it on.

That Panhead introduced me to the bikers' world. The first bikers I ever got to know were hardcore. Mark Lucas and Terry Rigsby owned and operated Tallahassee Motorcycle works. They did things to my bike I didn't yet know how to do. I went to the shop every chance I got. I learned so much from those two guys that they'll probably never know the impression they left on me. They taught me more than bikes—I learned about bikers and how to act. I learned how to show class. It has always meant a lot to me.

I struggled quite a bit to get my Pan on the road. It didn't want to run because the Zenith-Bendix carburetor was such a piece of shit. I will always hate them. Mine met its fate one day at the head of a sledgehammer, a fitting end to a miserable life. The first ride was sketchy, but I soon worked the bugs out of it. In just a few weeks of riding it, I met quite a cast of interesting characters that have left a remarkable imprint in my mind.

Panhead repair at the Buffalo Chip.

Author Photo

MoneyShot, the bike we built for the Camel Roadhouse tour, is the one thing in my life I've done that I'm the most proud of.

Because I didn't have a lot of money I made a lot of the parts myself. I made some of the more basic parts like the sissy bar, taillight, headlight, exhaust pipes, seat, and handlebar risers. That chopper got me into the motorcycle industry. People liked some of the parts I made, so I built parts for them. I took the money I made from selling parts and turned it back into a hobby that was rapidly becoming a business. I bought tools so I could build more bikes and make more parts.

My Pan was a real chopper. It was pretty neat, ahead of its time. It was hardcore, raw and simple. That's what choppers are—raw and simple. That chopper was real innovative. Admittedly, some of the bikes we build today at Choppers Inc. aren't really choppers; they're fabricated custom bikes. But I feel I can call the company by its name because it all evolved directly from my first chopper—a true chopper.

I made parts out of junk, shit that I found lying around. Ten years ago, people didn't understand what I was doing. When I built that first chopper, people didn't want anything to do with choppers, but I rode it all the time. If I had it today, people would say, "Wow, look at that thing. It's amazing." I rode the hell out of that bike and pretty much wore it out. The bike is in pieces now. It's still in my shop—Ruskin, my shop manager owns it now. I still look at it today and get ideas.

Everything I learned, I learned from building that one bike. I learned to fabricate, weld, and design by building that bike. I want to put that bike back together again some day to remind myself that building choppers is more than just a business, a payday. That bike reminds me that choppers are about freedom, power, and respect.

chapter TWO

Learning to Chop

I BUILT Choppers Inc. out of nothing. The first thing my business ever owned was what is inside my head and my 1950 Panhead. I have never had a credit line. When you look like me and walk into a bank, no one takes you seriously. I have, literally, built what I have from what is within. Every dime I made for a lot of years went back into Choppers Inc., except for the money that was absolutely necessary for my survival. I believed in my company so deeply that I knew it was my best investment. We still operate on our own cash, rather than borrowed money. When someone rips me off, I just laugh even though I'm pissed at getting burned, because I know that I'm just going to have to go back out in the shop and earn back what was taken from me. At different points in my life, I sold everything that ever meant anything to me to support and grow my business. That includes cars, motorcycles, and guns.

The front of our shop is as boring as what goes on inside is exciting.

When I first started, I worked out of my dad's garage with borrowed tools. I bought my 1950 Panhead, and that was my first experience in customizing. Once I had the bike mechanically solid, I started making custom parts for it. I couldn't afford the parts I wanted for my bike from the likes of Rick Doss, Donnie Smith, and Arlen Ness, so I started making the things I wanted on my own. I bought the tools and equipment I needed to make new parts, and learned how to use them through experience. The parts I created were sometimes crudely made, but that's how I learned. I really was my own first customer.

Author Photo

The Six-Gun

THOUGH IT WOULD STILL BE A FEW YEARS before I formally incorporated Choppers Inc., everything I did after building my first chopper was focused on turning chopper building into a business. I got into manufacturing parts almost right away. I was still in college when I developed the six-gun stuff, back in 1994 or 1995. I didn't know how to use a lathe or a mill, so I went and bought a Smithy machine, a combination lathe and mill. I learned to use it to make spacers and other necessary parts. While I was using the machine to make functional parts, I realized I could use it to make ornamental parts. I started making stuff for my family and friends because I didn't have any money. I invested every cent I made into buying tools and parts for building more choppers. The first six-gun piece was an oil cap I made for my buddy Jean-Luc. It's really different from the pieces I make today.

From what I've seen most bikers are into the same things—booze, bikes, women, guns.

People saw the six-gun oil cap and they wanted it.

There are so many round parts on a motorcycle that are natural places for the six-gun design.

People saw the six-gun oil cap and they wanted it. I started making six-gun risers and end caps and people would say, "Wow, where can I get that?" From what I've seen most bikers are into the same things—booze, bikes, women, guns. I'm into all those things. I'm into booze and women and I'm into guns and motorcycles. I don't care if a bike has a windshield or a fucking baby seat on the back; every motorcycle makes some kind of a statement. But a bagger makes a very different statement than a chopper. The six-gun parts work on choppers because they make the same statement choppers make: "Hey, don't fuck with me. I just might shoot your ass."

There are so many round parts on a motorcycle that are natural places for the six-gun design. I made a lot of functional six-gun parts. Now other people are making similar products. People are making all kinds of crazy six-gun shit but a lot of it doesn't make any sense. A lot of it is useless, like the chrome "live to ride, ride to live" badges people glue all over their baggers in an attempt to make their bikes stand out from the hundreds of thousands of identical baggers you see on the road every day. I've heard there is an ass for every seat, but my ass doesn't belong on a bagger's seat. Early one-percenter clubs called baggers garbage-wagons. They were frowned upon, and usually prohibited. If I wanted comfort, I'd buy a Volvo.

Getting Serious

AT FIRST I built choppers just for my own rides, but soon I was building bikes for other people. On the surface this wouldn't have seemed like a good time to start building choppers for a living. The public's taste ran either towards heavy bikes with elaborate body work—the polar opposites of choppers—or towards the retro bikes Harley was producing at its factories. Back then everyone wanted a new Harley. Through the mid-1990s, people were waiting for new Harleys for over a year because demand was greater than the supply the factory was capable of cranking out. People were paying exorbitant prices for bikes at the dealerships.

I didn't care. I loved choppers, so choppers were what I lived and built. Choppers were cheap because nobody wanted them, and they were considered obsolete and out of style. In the eyes of the magazines and all but a few key people in the aftermarket parts industry, choppers were not cool. But that's not how I saw it.

A few big name guys were still building choppers with lots of style, like C&L Hog Shop's legendary Lou Falcigno. I was able to relate to him and other chopper guys. They were working on bikes that I could afford, but taking the styling to a whole new level. My business evolved from that, and by the late 1990s people were starting to pay attention to my work.

The six-gun parts work on choppers because they make the same statement choppers make.

Fat Rubber

THE FIRST COMMERCIALLY SUCCESSFUL parts I manufactured were wide wheels for fat tires. The timing was perfect. In the mid-1990s, Metzeler Tires came out with the 200mm wide tire that was the biggest thing anyone had ever seen. Prior to that time, builders and customizers including myself were using 180mm tires from Japanese sportbikes to achieve the wide rear look on our bikes. Innovators like Donnie Smith created products such as his X-Drive wide swingarm kit, which made it possible to put a wider tire on a Harley-Davidson Softail. I couldn't afford a Softail back then, and I wouldn't have been able to afford an X-Drive kit either.

I wanted to put that big Metzeler tire on my Panhead, but nobody made a frame wide enough to accept a tire wider than a 180mm Avon. I couldn't afford the money to buy a wider rim for a bigger tire so I decided to make my own wheels.

It began at a junkyard my friend Mark owns in Opa Locka, near Miami. I bought a set of factory rims off a Ford Econoline van. They were 15 inches in diameter and 8 1/2 inches wide. I cut the centers out of them with an oxygen-acetylene torch, ground out the slag, and drilled holes in the rim for the spokes from a jig I made, copying the spoke pattern from a narrower motorcycle rim. I laced the rim to a stock Harley-Davidson hub with stock spokes. I eventually found an easier way to manufacture the wheels, but the rough start paid off. They were the widest rims anyone had ever seen on a custom bike, and they were impressive to see with the 200mm Metzeler tire mounted on them. That's when I met the guys from the then-new *Horse* magazine in Sturgis in 1997. *The Horse* is the successor to the famous underground magazine *Iron Horse*. The staff at *The Horse* offered to shoot our bikes for magazine features and showcase my products, and I offered to write tech and how-to articles for them.

The first *Horse* photo shoot at my shop turned into a high-speed frenzy featuring two models loaded on pills, lots of booze, and permanent damage to Warren's Snap-On toolbox. The photographer panicked and left before we were done. I am pretty sure I left an impression. Whether that impression was good or bad, I can't say, but I was their first advertiser. We believed in each other, and they are a huge part of my success. I'd like to think we've helped each other equally.

The Money Magnet

THE BIKE THAT really got things going was the Money Magnet. Due to the popularity of that bike I started to see an increase in the amount of money people were willing to spend with me. Before that I was selling bikes for $15,000 or $20,000. After Money Magnet I started selling bikes for $30,000 or $40,000. That was nearly twice the price of a stock Harley at the time. Hence the name "Money Magnet."

I borrowed the money to build the bike from my father. Dad was reluctant to lend me the $4,500 asking price but he did. I hadn't been building customs for that long then, and I don't think he was able to see where I would take things if I had the right opportunities. The bike was a 1972 Shovelhead in a Paughco rigid frame, and it ran good. The two previous owners were friends of mine, and I'd worked on the bike many times. I knew it was a good machine, and saw in it the potential for something big. There is a chopper beneath the surface of every Harley-Davidson, I think, and this one was no different.

Money Magnet

At the time, I had already built two custom bikes and was working on two more. They weren't really the style I liked, but I had to do what I had to do to get by. I knew in my mind that I wanted this bike to resemble the long choppers popular in Sweden, but it would have to be more refined aesthetically. I liked the Swedish style, but always felt the European bikes were just a little too industrial in their approach.

I used to flip through the old biker magazines when I would visit Tallahassee Motorcycle Works while I was in college. I remembered seeing some of Pat Kennedy's work and liking his style and the way he used some trick old engine designs with dual carburetor cylinder heads. I definitely wanted to do something crazy with the heads, because I hadn't seen any of that done in any of the recent issues of the magazines.

I was low on money and equipment so I convinced Bob, my then-girlfriend Claudia's dad, to rake and stretch the frame for me. Bob is an excellent machinist, sheet-metal fabricator, and welder, and I knew he could handle the job. The frame of the bike was stretched 4 inches and I moved the seat back 5 inches, creating quite a reach to the bars for a rider my size. Bob also did the work on the rear cylinder head to relocate the exhaust port toward the primary side of the bike. I used two Linkert M-74B carbs because I liked the way they looked and I got them for free.

I widened the frame to fit Avon's 230mm tire, which had just been released. I mounted the tire on a Ford van rim that I bought at a junkyard for fifteen dollars. A few companies were making frames for 200mm tires, but they were only built to handle those tires on 5-inch-wide rims. The 8.5 inchers that I was using wouldn't fit and, besides, I couldn't have afforded one of those frames. I built a jig, cut the rear end off behind the transmission mount and seat-post, and widened it 4 inches. I moved the transmission over to the left side of the bike so that the drive

Knuckle Sandwich

chain would clear the wider rim and tire and I made a primary drive spacer to offset the primary belt, since the pulley and clutches moved outboard with the transmission. I removed the rear brake rotor from the right side of the wheel hub and placed it and the brake caliper on the left side instead, inboard of the rear drive sprocket. The rear fender is actually a Knucklehead front fender that I widened. I got it for free too.

The fork sliders came from my friend Ed Odom's 1958 rigid Panhead. They were frozen to the fork tubes when Eddie owned the bike, making it an excruciating ride. We mounted a used early Wide Glide front end on Ed's Pan, and he gave me the sliders for free. I hand-machined the inboard disc brake system, locating the caliper and rotor inboard of the sprocket and drive chain. This approximated the early drum-brake look with better stopping power. The front wheel cost me $35 at a swap meet in Daytona Beach during Bike Week.

I made the exhaust pipes from the bends of old throw-away factory pipes, and I made the oil tank from sheet metal that Bob boosted from his metal shop's scrap pile. We used a peanut gas tank that I bought at the swaps and stretched. The handlebars were made from an old set of cast-off drag bars that had been cut, mitered, flipped, and welded together. I was so loaded on Jack Daniels and Budweiser the night I made the handlebars and gas tank that I named them Whiskey Bars and Longneck Tanks, respectively.

I took the unfinished bike to the Indianapolis Powersports Expo in early 1998, and people were blown away. There was nothing like it there, and everyone wanted to know who the punk-ass kid in his twenties was and where he got those parts. It felt good. Chopper builders Jesse James and Rick Doss were at the show and both liked my work, even though the bike was unfinished. That day Rick told me I would go places and I hope, someday, to prove that he was right. Jesse took particular interest in the six-gun gas cap, handlebar risers, and oil cap that

I made by hand. He invited me to his first annual No Love Party and I brought him a pair of risers as a thank-you gift. We've been friends since we met, and he is the only person I've ever licensed or even allowed to use my six-gun designs. Many people have copied them illegally and without my consent. I feel that Jesse has earned it, and he has returned the favor to me fully. Everyone else who has tried to use them can fuck off.

There is a huge aftermarket for wide tire bikes and parts today, with hundreds of companies and thousands of parts that make it easy for customizers to run wide wheels and tires. The Money Magnet was there on the floor before all of them. Money Magnet is a true chopper, because I chopped off the garbage and either threw it away, or made something new and useful out of it. I had the opportunity to buy it back recently, but declined because it was in another state and the sale had to be immediate. I wonder if I made a mistake?

Incorporating

WE INCORPORATED Choppers Inc. in 1998. I had wanted to name my business Choppers Inc. ever since 1992 or 1993. I had come back from a night of riding and partying on South Beach and watched *Murder Inc.* on television. That's where I got the idea for the name. I remember the suicide doors of the old Ford Sedan in the film swinging open, and gangsters in suits with Tommy guns shooting up a restaurant. It was a powerful scene that left its mark, and I rolled it all into the name of my company. I planned to become powerful myself, and leave my own mark.

I'd been building bikes at an underground level for about four years by the time we incorporated. I didn't take it that seriously at first, but then I realized that I was getting older and had to quit fucking around. I was tired of all the bullshit trouble with the cops in South Florida.

One detective in particular made a career of going after Warren. He had a hard-on for Warren because Warren told him to fuck off at least one time. The cop was a real cowboy. I won't mention his name, as a favor. I feel he owes me one now. The one time he busted Warren (and me), Warren wasn't even involved in Choppers, Inc.

In 1997 Warren sold some frames to a friend who was a professional crook. The guy used the frame numbers to launder stolen bikes. The guy got busted and rolled over on us. He tried to pin the stolen bikes on Warren and me. I was the one with the business and building. I was the one who took the hit.

I was getting ready to go to Sturgis when the cops came. They pulled up to our place with two vans and six flatbed trucks, determined to seize my property. They cut the chains off our fence and busted in, uninvited. They cleaned out my shop, took all my tools, all my guns, all my six-gun parts, all my bikes, and all my parts. They took everything.

The prosecutor was a young, fresh county attorney, wet behind the ears. She believed everything cowboy cop said. I went through it real hard, real fucking hard, but we were never charged with anything. They did try to indict me for making illegal firearms—they thought my six-gun chopper parts were for real guns. They finally figured out that the charge was idiotic, but I still nearly lost everything.

Rolling chassis' waiting to be shipped.

Jennifer Schneider

When I went to claim my stuff, they said they couldn't find any documentation that the stuff belonged to me. They had misplaced all the paperwork. I'd made copies of everything so I could prove it belonged to me. I was able to get most of it back. I guess there's a fine line between some cops and thieves. They have that kind of power.

It took me about eight or nine months to get my stuff back. After Sturgis in 1998 I got home, slept for a couple of days, woke up, threw my shit in my truck and moved to Melbourne.

I had problems with working in Miami. They wouldn't let us have any signage. They wouldn't let us do business. They thought I was some kind of big-ass criminal. They said I was known to associate with motorcycle "gangs."

Miami was all cops and robbers. If you weren't one, they thought you were the other. In Melbourne they still gave me a little bit of a hassle at first. I was greeted with skepticism. There was word from Miami that I was trouble. When I went to get a bike titled, they'd go over the numbers and give me a little bit of shit—it was just cops being cops—but you can do business in Melbourne. In Miami you had the city, the county, and the EPA crawling up your ass all the time. Melbourne finally threw me the welcome mat, and there aren't many other places I'd rather live.

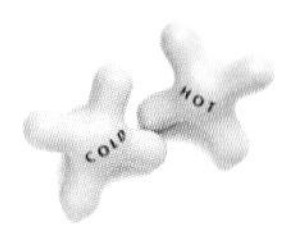

Ruskin Passaro

Hiring employees

I KNEW I NEEDED A PARTNER to succeed. My cousin was my partner but I think we had different ambitions. Then I had a partner named Joey. Our ambitions also differed. Then I was partners with my brother Warren for a while, but that didn't work out. We struggled because our ambitions were different as well. I was the common denominator, so I decided it was best I move on. I offered to give Warren my half of the business and walk away from it but he didn't want to do that. He told me I could just have his half but I refused. In the end, I gave him a fair price for his half. The only valuable part of the business at that point was what was inside my head. To me any price would be a good price for that information.

We hired Nick Fredella in 1998 or 1999. He worked with us for a few months, but I couldn't afford to pay him what he was worth. Nick found a well-paying job that, eventually, nearly took his life. As unfortunate as those circumstances were, they were the springboard for the working relationship we have today. He came back in 2001 to work for me exclusively full time as a subcontractor. Nick and I became friends almost as accidentally as he came to work for me. I had just met Ruskin and was working out of warehouse space that I rented from him. Nick came in one day while I was working on my bike and started talking to me about high school and racing cars. Nick is six years older than me, and I was pretty confused at first. I finally realized that Nick knew my older brother, whom I resemble, and had mistaken me for him. When I stood up to grab another beer, Nick realized his mistake. Warren is three inches taller than me. We laughed, but it has been beer and bikes for Nick and me since that day. I can't imagine my business without him present.

Nick Fredella

Jennifer at work.

Right now we have eight people working full time. We hired Ruskin Passaro as general manager in 2003. He was a little shady when I met him. He hustled, buying and selling whatever would bring him cash. But his hustle is strong, and it has helped him make it in life. He knows the rules of the street. He knows how to handle people who fuck you over. He was a little rough at first. He'd tell people, "Fuck you. You're done." When you grow up on the streets, you don't learn a lot of diplomacy. He's learning it now. He's a good guy. I know his mom. She's brought him up right, and I'm proud of her for it. She reminds me of my mother. Ruskin's strengths are my weaknesses. I used to operate my business and run my life so that virtually no one had the opportunity to fuck me over, but that was on the street. In the straight world of legitimate business, we all have our vulnerabilities. Ruskin's really, really sharp about dealing with that mess.

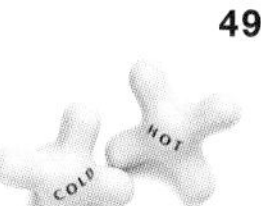

I can rely on Ruskin. I delegate work to him and he does it. I don't have to keep asking him and asking him and asking him. When I ask him once, it gets done without excuses. I've never before had that in the management end of my business.

I hired Jennifer Schneider as my personal assistant in June 2003. I decided I needed a personal assistant the year before, when I was in Sturgis at the Camel tent hanging out with Bill Dodge and Jesse James and people were just mobbing Jesse. He was getting frustrated because

I've been lucky to have some great friends like Bean're.

people were fucking crazy. He said, "Hey man, I got to get out of here." Jesse nodded at Renee, his personal assistant, and the deal was done that very moment. Jesse didn't have to ask Renee any questions—she gave him all the information he needed. Soon there was a car coming to pick him up. I said to myself, I got to get someone to do that for me—I need a Renee. Jennifer is it.

Jennifer worked for the Camel Roadhouse Tour, arguably the most well known and prestigious entity in the custom motorcycle world during its existence. When Camel cut The Roadhouse Tour, Jennifer was out of a job. I called her and asked her what she'd been doing. She said, "Nothing. I've been drinking for two weeks." I thought that if she'd been drinking for two weeks she'd fit right in with my company. As with many things, I don't know how I was able to function prior to having

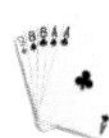

Jennifer on board. She is highly intelligent, organized, young, attractive, and well-mannered. She fits right into my company's lifestyle.

We've got a good organization. I give them a good place to work and they give me a good place to work. Ruskin is getting my business very organized and running it like a business so that there's no confusion. He makes sure everyone knows what their job is. It helps to keep people with us. He was smart enough to hire an assistant, Tammy, to help him with his enormous responsibilities. Nick is becoming one hell of a fabricator, and I'm more proud of him than he knows. I hope to teach him everything I know, and I'm still learning. Jen keeps me straight and organized, which I really need. Most days I'm so overwhelmed, and she's there to keep me on time. Carlos, Dave Deluxe, and Forest handle our inventory and orders. I feel like the whole company is its own core. Everything is critical when you are this close to the top.

Building Bikes

WE PLAN TO BUILD 10 bikes in 2004. We built six last year. In 2001 we built 26 bikes and that was a disaster. It almost killed the business. We didn't have the resources to build that many bikes and quality suffered. I was bringing money in hand over fist—we were building expensive bikes—but we didn't have the infrastructure to do what we were trying to do. We weren't screening our customers properly. Every customer we had owed me money. There's a lot of overhead in building bikes, and people weren't paying us. A lot of people still owe me money.

Now people pay me up front. I won't build a bike unless it's paid for. When I want something, I pay for it. I expect the same from my customers. One of the ways people try to get out of paying for something is to say, "Hey, I don't like what you did." When someone starts pulling that shit, you know he's never going to pay you. We ended up spending all our money on lawyers. Lawyers don't work for you if you don't pay them.

So we said, "Wait a minute. Let's slow this train down. Let's pick our customers." We'd rather have ten customers with real money than 100 people with Rolexes and expensive cars and notepads full of excuses and stacks of unpaid bills. We said let's redirect the business. Let's focus on parts so we get paid for what we do. We dropped the number of bikes we build and raised our quality.

Last year we almost shut down totally to work on the Discovery Channel's *Biker Build-Off* shows. We only built six bikes last year.

I've always said that the best bikes we've ever built were the ones I did for myself. The Money Magnet, Blue, Devil-in-a-Red-Dress, PsychoBilly Cadillac, MoneyShot, VQ Bike, and WholeLottaRosie were all built for me to my liking. MissBehavin' always belonged to Ruskin, but he allowed me to do whatever the hell I wanted to with it. I'd kill to have that gas tank back. I left out the Orange Discovery Channel bike because I never really liked it. I seem to be in the minority on that, but it's the way I feel.

I haven't raised my prices since we've been on television. If you come to me and want a bike, I'm going to charge a fair price for it and I'm going to build it. That's why my hands are always dirty. Now I only have six or ten shots each year to impress the customers so I have to make each bike an expression of my vision of what a chopper should be.

I'm getting better every day. I'm becoming more patient and more resilient. I'm becoming fully intolerant of sloppy work. It is misunderstood in my shop sometimes for arrogance, but I want each of my bikes to be flawless. My name is on them.

PsychoBilly Cadillac

Suppliers and Outsourcing

MY STRENGTH IS THAT I'm a creator and an innovator. Management, manufacturing, and distribution do not interest me in the least. I try to organize the business so that I can focus on creating and innovating. We try to subcontract things that detract from my creativity. From engineering, I understand manufacturing processes. I'm able to create a product and communicate with a manufacturer in a way that keeps the product cost down and also enables easy production and distribution. I don't design sophisticated, hard-to-use parts. People don't understand complicated parts. I don't fully understand how my laptop computer works, and I don't want to know. I keep things simple. Choppers, by nature, are supposed to be simple.

All of this, of course, causes problems. We tried to outsource our website and we got screwed. I spent $18,000 to have someone design it, and the fucking website still doesn't work. I tried to get something changed. It doesn't happen. That was the most dissatisfying purchase I've ever made in my life.

Peterbilt

I paid three times what my website is actually worth, because I trusted the web development company. It has never worked properly since we launched it. All I've ever gotten is excuses. I told the woman who owns the company that I have never been as disappointed with any purchase in my life as I am with the one I made with her company. She didn't care when I said it. I now have a completely new website.

57

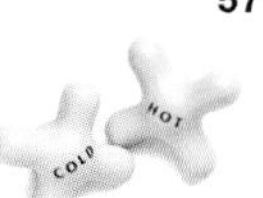

I thought she might possibly be the greediest person I would have to deal with, but I was way wrong. That honor belongs to the folks at an anonymous clothing manufacturer. We tried to outsource the clothing manufacturing and we got fucked. I sat across the table from the assholes who run the company and told them how I'd been fucked just recently by one of their neighboring clothing companies. They swore to me that they would never do me the same, that they had my company's best interests at heart. They told me what they could and would do for me until they were blue in the face. All I wanted them to know was what I wouldn't tolerate. Smiles around the room. I would have loved to have been a fly on the wall in that room after I got up and left. They must have winked and smiled, because they intended to fuck me all along. And they did. Those bastards have even gone so far as to try to trademark my company's name with the United States Patent and Trademark Office. I have no sympathy for people too cowardly to go out and make an honest living.

The worst thing is that when suppliers let us down, we end up letting our customers down. I'm making promises to people. They're expecting things from me. My website troubles caused us to be

back ordered with clothing for over a year at one point, and that clothing company has cost a lot of honest business people who were banking on selling our product huge money. Recently I had several store owners complain that they were losing business because of supply problems with our clothes. One company's greed can hurt so many honest people. It's not the American way.

In the Wind

I THINK A LOT OF PEOPLE in the motorcycle industry don't have a real love of motorcycling. There are many people who do, but the number of those in it just for the money is inordinate. In too many cases I think the lifestyle left the industry and it got to be about anything and everything but fun shit. It's time for us all to watch *Easy Rider* one more time. One of the reasons I value my friends that are one percenters so much is because they genuinely love their bikes, and love to kick it with other people who love their bikes. Commercialization has ruined much of the climate that existed even back when I got into all of this. I think a lot of custom builders are in it just for the publicity, to get into magazines and be on television. I might seem hypocritical for stating this, but every time someone asks me how to get on the Discovery Channel, I want to ask them if they know how to flash the field on a generator. Do they know how many needle bearings are in an early four-speed transmission, or how to properly set up a mousetrap? Anyone who claims to be a chopper builder and doesn't know what a mousetrap is deserves a size 10 1/2 boot in the ass and certainly doesn't know what a chopper is.

PsychoBilly Cadillac when it was coming together.

I feel protective of the fun. I truly love motorcycling. I think that shows in bikes like my bobbers. I don't build bikes like that for the money. I can't use any of the products I sell on bikes like that. I build bikes like that because I love them.

A lot of builders and mechanics who don't ride much run into trouble with their bikes breaking. You figure things out when you ride all the time. That's why we engineer our motor mounts to be strong—I don't like motor mounts breaking when I'm on a 500-mile ride. We use heavy frame tubing for our license plate brackets so our license plates don't vibrate off. Everything we do, we do with riding in mind. Yes, I want my work to look good, but nobody looks good stuck on the side of the road.

One of the problems I ran into with my first Panhead was the exhaust pipes falling off. On a Panhead the pipes just slip on and they don't stay on very well. I like my bikes to look nice and they didn't look all that nice when the pipes would fall off and get all beat up. They'd fall off and that cost me a lot of money at a time when I didn't have a lot of money. Now I weld billet exhaust-pipe mounts to the frame. I mount the pipes in a couple of different places and never have to worry about exhaust pipes coming off. If you can't lift your bike by grabbing its exhaust pipes, the mounts aren't strong enough. They should be strong enough to support the weight of the bike

Old School Design and the Hubless Bikes

Of all the bikes we've built so far, we're perhaps best known for the hubless bikes—PsychoBilly Cadillac and MoneyShot, the bike we built for the Camel Roadhouse tour. The technology for the hubless bikes dates back to the 1960s. It was not my concept. I was just the guy who said, "Let's do it." The hubless bike is fantasy technology, like *Star Wars*. I used to watch *Star Wars*, watch the doors automatically open and think, "No fucking way." Now every grocery store has doors that open automatically.

Author Photo

Choppers Inc. is perhaps best known for our hubless bikes.

In Denver with Joey Perse, examining the parts that make the hubless bikes work. Joey owns the shop with all the cool shit we need to build the hubless bikes.

Who knows what kind of crazy shit Joey and I were cooking up when Michael took this photo?

There had been a hubless design before. A guy named Franco Sbarro built a hubless concept bike in the late 1980s. I never even knew of him until I'd already built the PsychoBilly Cadillac. Our designs differ greatly, and mine actually works. I thought of a type of bearing that would make it possible and searched for over a year for just the right bearing. I almost gave up, and then I ran across a company that designed bearings for a helicopter company. The bearings were just what I needed to make a rideable hubless bike. They cost over $8,000 apiece, but they are perfect.

Getting the gearing right was a challenge, but we got it to work really well. I would have liked to have used a two-tooth smaller rear sprocket on the MoneyShot bike, but I would have had to use smaller bolts to mount the sprocket to the rim. I did the math and the smaller bolts wouldn't have been strong enough. Still, it's totally rideable.

MoneyShot

I truly love motorcycling. I think that shows in my bikes.

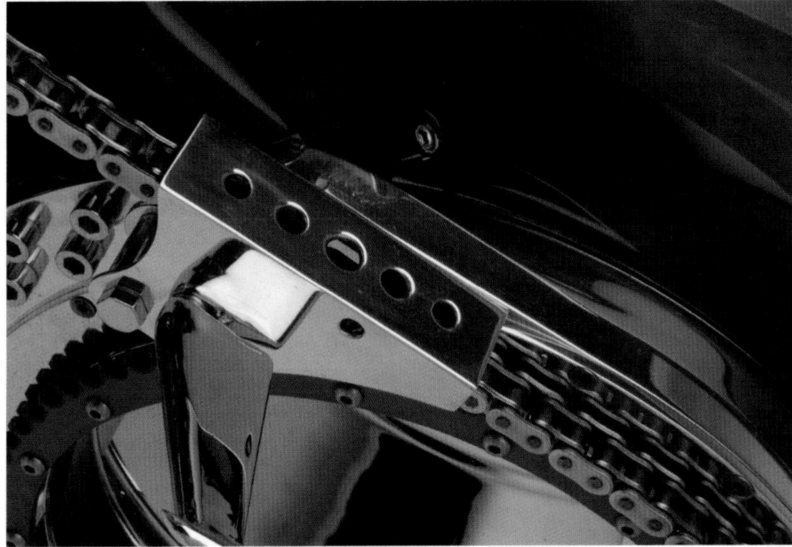

People ask me when will I build a hubless front wheel. A hubless front wheel is easy to build—it's the back wheel that's difficult. I'll never build a hubless front wheel. A wannabe famous builder from Tennessee just recently unveiled his hubless front and rear wheel bike. I don't believe it's fully functional, but he's trying to build his reputation off of it. He shamelessly took out an ad in one of the major cycle magazines a year ago announcing his creation, while also claiming to have created almost every style and trick currently out there. I thought, "What a bitch." The guy's ego is so big, and his confidence is so low, that he has to resort to this.

My friend Morray once showed me a piece of memorabilia that was given to him as a gift from the Outlaws Motorcycle Club. It reads, "Everything you ever wanted to be, I already am." I think that to myself every time I see someone trying to rip my game. My bitch from Tennessee definitely falls right in line. So you'll never see me doing a front hubless wheel. It's been done, and I'm an originator.

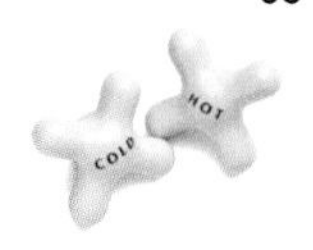

Paul Cox seat on MoneyShot.

Peterbilt

chapter THREE

INSPIRATION

Mondo Porras and I riding in the spring of 2004.

LOOKING at the *Easyriders* magazines with my brother, I began associating choppers with freedom. We had a very strict upbringing. We weren't allowed to have long hair, we were expected to behave in a certain way. Bikers would pull up and my parents would pull me away. In the magazines I saw all these people riding bikes and smoking marijuana pipes, ads for grow lights and paraphernalia, all the stuff I was told I couldn't do. When I got older I realized I could look the way I wanted to. Now I pull up someplace and people pull their kids away from me.

Riding a chopper and the image that comes with it has its drawbacks. Cops give me a hard time. Cops act like we have no rights but we do. They want to search my shit all the time and I tell them they can't. And they can't. That just makes them want to search my shit even more, but I know I have to keep my rights. I travel light with just the bare necessities because eventually they are going to get a search warrant and search my shit, but I make them do it the right way.

Sometimes I have to get out and ride, even when I have other things I'm supposed to be doing. It clears my head.

In the spring of 2004, I had a run-in with the law enforcement people at the Laughlin River Run in Nevada. Mondo Porras and I were heading across the river, to Bullhead City, to visit a friend in need. We would never make it, thanks to some prick police officers. My 1948 Panhead ran out of gas on Casino Drive around 9:00 a.m., about 100 feet from a gas station. I pushed my bike off to the side of the road, not sure just yet if there was a mechanical problem or if it was out of fuel. About thirty seconds later a patrol car pulled up next to me and told me to get out of the road. I'm a recognizable guy, and a crowd had already gathered around me. People wanted pictures, and I just wanted to get some gas and ride with my friend. I had a hard time hearing the cop, since he was too lazy to get out of his car. But I knew what he wanted, and I complied. I pushed my bike off into a parking lot driveway, as he barked commands from his window.

I know how to act, but I don't tolerate disrespect. This cop pushed me in a corner to get me to fight, and I wasn't going to have it. He lost his cool, and opened the door and started running toward me from his car. It was very windy, and his gay baseball cap blew off his head. I couldn't help myself at this point so I offered him some advice. I said, "Why don't you go get your fuckin' hat and leave me the fuck alone?" I look great in handcuffs, and you know the rest. There were many witnesses to all of this that morning, and they really gave the police a hard time. Rightly so. I thank all of those people for their support. What happened was bullshit and cowardly.

Ever since I was a kid, I associated riding choppers with freedom.

I was arrested for impeding traffic, something typically dealt with by issuing a warning or a simple traffic ticket. I was taken to jail and booked. I have got to say that the booking officers and everyone else at the station were polite and professional. They were surprised that I was arrested for such a violation and asked why I didn't offer bail on the spot. I had more than enough cash in my pocket at the time of my arrest. It turns out that the arresting officer is able to exercise discretion, no matter how poor that discretion may be, on whether to release me on bail. He insisted I stay the afternoon and go on the bus to Las Vegas central booking later in the evening. That meant I would be forced to go the ninety miles to Vegas, and I wouldn't even be able to make bail until around 9:00 p.m. What a ball-breaker.

Several friends of mine, who are good cops, saw and heard what happened to me. They called the station and talked to the sergeant in charge. He came in and explained to me that they would possibly allow me to make bail in Laughlin, if I agreed to quit antagonizing his soldiers. I'd already found the time to do 200 push-ups and 300 sit-ups, so I agreed. By the time they were ready to return my property and release me, I had also learned how to break out of a set of handcuffs. That college education was worth the effort.

It's hard not to attract attention when you're riding a chopper. Sometimes you attract the wrong kind of attention.

Riding with Ron Finch from Kansas City to Vegas.

Freedom and the Need for Speed

TO ME, the late artist and customizer Von Dutch represents the essence of American freedom. He has been a huge influence on me. He had a lot of opportunities. He had a lot of shit thrown at him, but he said, "No, I'm going to do what I want to do." He was an artist. He didn't do things the way other people wanted him to do them. He lived by his principles and not by what made him money. Now his name is being exploited by anyone and everyone who can get their hands on it. Anna Nicole Smith wears Von Dutch clothing and she doesn't even know there was a person named Von Dutch. I figure the best way to honor him is to carry on his style without applying his name to it in a cheap way. You can see his vision in what I do, but I haven't made him my whore.

People ask me how they can get into the business. I tell them, "Go buy a bike and start working on it." That's how I did it. I'm still doing the same shit today. If I see an old bike, I buy it and work on it. It doesn't take $50,000 to build a cool bike. You just have to do it.

CLUB CASTINGS
DE LUXE

MILWAUKEE
LICENSED
TAXICAB DRIVER
1335
EXPIRES JUNE 30
1969

I use found art on my choppers whenever I can. Sometimes a piece of junk you pick up at a swap meet can look as cool on a chopper as a $5,000 custom-built piece.

I use found art. I take something that belongs to something else and put it on a bike. This stuff is free or very cheap and it looks cool on a $50,000 custom bike. But you can't just start sticking shit on a bike and expect it to look cool. You have to have a vision of how the bike will look when it's finished before you start. But once you have that vision, it doesn't matter if the part cost $1,000, $1, or if it was free, as long as it helps you make your vision a reality.

There's nothing wrong with buying a cool $50,000 bike if you can afford it, but not everyone can afford it. We'll keep building cool $50,000 bikes as long as people keep buying them, but the bikes I build will inspire people who can't afford something like that to go out and build their own choppers. I want them to buy an old Panhead or Shovelhead and see what they can do with it themselves. We sell a lot of great parts people can use to customize their bikes, but the really special choppers will be the ones that express the builder's own imagination. I know for a fact that if you can imagine it, it can be built. The only thing holding people back is a lack of imagination.

When I first got interested in bikes in the late 1980s, Arlen Ness, Donnie Smith, Arlin Fatland, and Dave Perewitz had their Hamster scene going. There were guys like Ron Finch and Lou Falcigno who weren't getting as much publicity as they deserved, but they were pounding, cutting, and bending metal like there would be no tomorrow. The Hamsters were dominating the industry. My ratty old Panhead was a real low-budget chopper. Everything on their bikes was perfect. I really admired that. But I really liked their older stuff. I was heavily influenced by their early work. I saw their stuff in old magazines and it set me on fire. It inspired me.

"Tasty Glass" by Billy Velvet.

Arlen Ness and Building a Career

YOU MEET THE SAME PEOPLE on the way up as you do on the way down. My goal is that when I do come back down I will have climbed high enough to still be at a workable level when I fall. I'm building a foundation with my business that I hope will keep me from falling below a certain level. Even if *Easyriders* doesn't like my bikes anymore I still have the parts business to fall back on. That's one of the reasons Arlen Ness is such a huge influence on me. My bikes are very different from his, but I try to pattern my career on his.

Arlen's development of his parts business is one of the smartest things anyone in this industry has ever done. I asked Dave Perewitz why he's never gotten into the parts business. He said, "I don't know. I just never did." Same with Arlin Fatland. He never started a parts business. What Arlen Ness has done—built an industry from building motorcycle parts—is amazing. He's literally built a brand out of nothing but his good name. It's pretty trippy.

Arlen was a painter—he started spraying on people's bikes. You know that the first time he laid some paint on someone's bike he wasn't thinking, "I'm going to build an empire out of this." Arlen doesn't have a big head. He doesn't walk around thinking that his success was his birthright. He earned it. He's a good lesson in humility for us younger guys.

Arlen Ness and Dave Perewitz had done some wild stuff in the 1970s and 1980s. I loved their craftsmanship, but wasn't all that crazy about their style. It was their old work that held my interest. Mike Lichter's motorcycle exhibit at the Journey Museum in Rapid City during the Sturgis Rally a couple of years ago included 13 of Arlen's bikes across the decades. I was impressed to see some of the creations I'd drooled over on magazine pages in person. Arlen is a humble and quiet guy, but his bikes are anything but that. I stared at his work for a couple of hours, in awe. That guy is the Elvis Presley of custom motorcycles. Beyond that, he has created the industry standard for custom builders who want to turn their one-off creations into products for the public.

I've been successful doing what I learned from Arlen Ness: hand-making a part for a custom bike, then mass producing it and marketing it as a means of income. If I can't show up to work for a week, we still make money. And people who cannot afford one of my bikes can have some element of what I do on their own ride, thanks to Arlen's business model. It's nice.

Arlen was present on the set of *Big,* which we recently filmed in California. I've talked to him before, but never on the level we did during the shoot. I'm hard to impress, but he did it easily. There is one person who truly does love motorcycles and the biker lifestyle.

Donnie Smith

I MISSED MY FLIGHT to the Donnie Smith Invitational show in St. Paul, Minnesota in 2004. I really wanted to go, but I missed my plane by one minute. We'd just finished an *Easyriders* bike show in Denver, and I got shook down in airport security as usual.

Anyone who can host their own bike show of the magnitude of Donnie's show has got to have it going on. Donnie's a great guy. He was quoted in a magazine article saying something about the bike I built for the Discovery Channel's *Biker Build-Off II* not being right, that it was crooked. I talked to him and I said, "You know what? You were right. There was shit wrong with the bike. I appreciate that you had the balls to say it. I'm glad you didn't sugar coat it."

Donnie's quote was included in a Beau Allen Pacheco article in *American Rider*, which poorly chronicled *Biker Build-Off II*. Beau said some complimentary things about me that are appreciated, but wrote an inaccurate, biased, suggestive, and unobjective piece. That kind of bullshit is weak, but Donnie came right out and spoke his mind. I totally respect that. I also respect his work. Like any good artist, Donnie's work is unmistakably his. You know it when you see it. I mentioned his name to a younger, self-proclaimed master builder, and he mentioned that he'd never heard of Donnie Smith or seen his work. I felt like smacking him up. Donnie's work is painfully meticulous, something I wish mine was.

Dave Perewitz

WHEN BEAU ALLEN PACHECO interviewed me in Dallas at the *Easyriders* show in 2003, I said to him that "Dave Perewitz is four-star, I'm strip bar." Beau had asked me to compare my work with Dave's, and I gave him one of my candid responses. I'd been outside the show in the parking lot for a couple of hours drinking tequila and whiskey out of the bottle with a bunch of crazy Texans prior to saying it. I'd forgotten making that statement until I saw it in print. It's fitting.

Getting to know Dave through filming with the Discovery Channel was an unexpected gem. He is a person rich with intellect and history. His bikes are very refined and clean, like Arlen Ness' and Donnie Smith's. The three are contemporaries, and there are numerous similarities in the way they execute their work. However, they each have their own style, and Dave's is one of the most emulated.

Dave conducts himself with confidence and class, something I haven't seen from a lot of younger guys. People need to start paying attention to guys like Dave, Arlen, and Donnie—they have a lot to teach the rest of us.

Ron Finch

RON FINCH CALLED ME AFTER seeing me on the Discovery Channel, and at first I didn't believe that it was him on the phone when my assistant Jennifer told me who was calling. He has been an important influence on me. He's a legendary builder who avoided the limelight. His work has always been ahead of its time. Back when he focused his talent on motorcycles, people just didn't get it. That's where I was when I first started building bikes. At shows, people would say, "That's cool, but. . . ." They just didn't get it. It is extremely difficult to survive in an environment where everyone is trying to upstage the next guy. Originality doesn't flourish and Ron is nothing if not original. Ron is a risk taker, and it shows in his bikes. He took ornamental round steel rod work and incorporated it in a distinctive way. There is a very Art-Deco quality about what Ron does. His work is exceptional.

I had the pleasure of riding with Ron recently from Kansas City, Missouri, to the Viva Las Vegas hot rod car and rockabilly event. We rode, laughed, talked, and drank beer for a week. Ron's drinking abilities are legendary, like the man himself. I looked at his bike for hours as we rode alongside each other across the country, and I don't think I saw it all. Ron is an interesting guy with a lot to say. I learned a lot from him, and I know I have only touched the surface. He has been biking for longer than I have been breathing, and it shows. I was able to ask him questions I've always needed the answers to, and he offered the answers willingly and in great detail.

Pat Kennedy

PAT KENNEDY HAS BEEN ANOTHER huge influence on me. When everyone else was doing the rubber-mounted bikes, Pat Kennedy was building European-style long bikes. He was one of the few people still building actual choppers at a time when everyone else was fabricating custom bikes.

I like the fact that Pat's something of a recluse. He's not flashy. He's off doing his own thing. He's not always out at the shows. He's off at his place, kicking back. If someone offered him a television show, he'd probably turn it down. He picked his altitude and stayed at it. He doesn't want to soar to the top and he's not going to sink to the bottom. What he's doing with motorcycles is like what I do with surfing. When I surf, I just want to get out, drop into my wave. I'd like to be able to work like that.

Ralph "Sonny" Barger

WHETHER PEOPLE admit it or not, everyone interested in motorcycles and choppers has been influenced by Sonny Barger. He's one of the mythic figures of the twentieth century. He turned an outlaw motorcycle club into one of the most iconic cultural forces in America. He made bikes and his club his life, and he has paid for it in full.

I have a lot of respect for Sonny. The man has principles. Sometimes those principles might diverge from societal norms, but at least the man has principles, which is more than most people can say about themselves. He is what he is, and he's completely honest about that. I respect that about him. Being a biker is a way of life, and Sonny epitomizes the lifestyle.

Much of the way we bikers live is a direct result of what Sonny did with his club, and what other clubs have subsequently done. I've always said that bikers are a self-governing crowd, and that is due to the level and understanding of respect that the one percenters have established and insisted upon. I wish most people conducted themselves with the kind of integrity Sonny Barger has.

I build my bikes to ride, and Helle'sBelle is one of my favorites.

Willie Nelson

ALTHOUGH I've seen him play live in concert six times, the most recent Willie Nelson concert I attended is the one that left the most indelible mark. Willie reminded me of myself in many ways, and I sat and wondered if he'd experienced some of the same feelings I have on my way to where I am. I'd seen him play outdoors in the early 1990s with Waylon Jennings, on a huge sound stage with extensive lighting and stage equipment. But here we were, in a small auditorium of roughly five thousand people, watching and listening to his four-piece band back him up. Things had changed since the last time we shared company, and I thought about the time in between.

Willie Nelson was extremely famous, powerful, and successful long before I began showing up in Harley-Davidson chopper magazines. I never really recognized him for his fame; I appreciated him for his obvious talent. It took me a few years to understand that there was much more to his talent than was obvious, that achieving his level of success was, in and of itself, a talent. Willie Nelson existed and survived in a cutthroat industry where everyone was and is after his success, as long as it exists. His music was considered outlaw country music, like that of David Allan Coe and Waylon Jennings. Their music was never really fully accepted in the mainstream, and I think that's the way they all wanted it. That's what I always liked about it. They wouldn't want to be Garth Brooks.

VQ Bike

I remember the media frenzy surrounding Willie when the IRS began investigating his income tax reports, and it bothered me that so many people seemed so eager to see him struggle and fail. They wanted to use his celebrity to further their own ends, and it appeared un-American. I expected everyone to love him for the American Icon that he always will be, despite what someone might have dropped on him somewhere along the road. Over a lifetime of music, he has left us with a rich collection of artistic work that is distinctly his own. And that is all I strive to do.

Willie has strummed and plucked at the strings of the same six-string for so many years that his hand has worn a hole through the body of the guitar. The size of the hole has grown significantly since the first time I saw him play and sing. I knew what it was immediately when I first saw it, because I am also a guitar player, but I'd never played enough to make a mark like that on any of my instruments. By virtue of his work and his success, Willie's guitar has grown to be nearly as famous as he is, as much a part of his work as his lyrics and his melodies. He has left a mark that is widely recognized as undeniably his own. It is something that inspires and drives me. If the only result of all my years of work was that people recognized my work as my own, I would be satisfied.

I don't feel that I'm there yet, so I keep working at getting better at the only thing I know how to do. I'm going to keep building custom motorcycles and chopping ugly ones, and I'm going to just be me. Peter Fonda said it best in the movie *Easy Rider*: "You know, I never wanted to be anybody else."

David Mann

I HAVE ALWAYS ADMIRED the artwork of David Mann. He studied at Ed Roth's studios, and developed his own unique style of art. David's depictions of the biker lifestyle have, at times, been the most entertaining images in *Easyriders* magazine. We have always had David Mann's *Easyriders* centerfolds and posters adorning the walls in our shop, and I don't think I've ever been in a real custom motorcycle shop where I haven't seen at least one. Inherent in his work is his love of the lifestyle and the bikes that many of us adventurous riders have been lucky enough to know. He has captured it all completely and perfectly.

David Mann was inducted into the motorcycle Hall of Fame in 2004, and he deserved it. That is a huge honor for him, and it is as much of an honor for me to have been asked to personally induct him. David told me that he is a fan of my work, and that impressed me beyond words. To speak to someone I have admired so much for so long about what I do seems unnatural to me. There are a million questions I'd love to ask him and not nearly enough time to do so. That's the way it goes, sometimes. I'll take what I can get, and I think that may be more than I deserve. The man has made a difference.

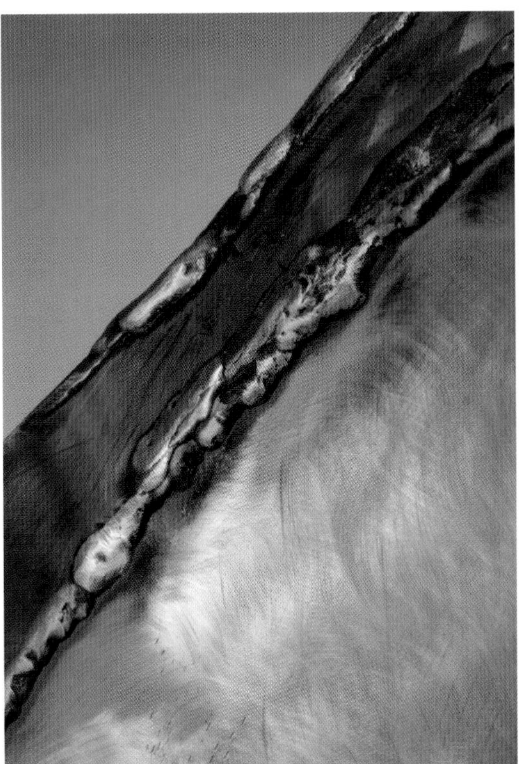

Jesse James and the New Breed of Chopper Builders

I HAD MET Jesse James at the Indianapolis Powersports Expo in 1998 when the Money Magnet wasn't finished, but Jesse saw it and liked it. I already knew who Jesse was. I was using his fenders on some of my bikes.

I met a lot of other young builders about the same time I met Jesse. There are only a few of us who have survived, like me, Jesse, and Matt Hotch. This goes to show you how hard it is to make it in this industry. Jesse's one of the survivors. Jesse's definitely one of my influences, not so much because of the bikes he builds—our bikes are very different—but he's influenced me as far as building the business.

One time at Sturgis, right after *Motorcycle Mania* came out, Jesse was being mobbed by a crowd. He looked at me and said, "You're next." *Motorcycle Mania* was a new thing. The only thing that had ever been on television about motorcycles was the history of Harley-Davidson. Jesse knew what to do and he pulled it off. He's been a role model for me.

Jesse's helped me a lot. The reason Jesse asked me to be part of the first episode filmed of *Monster Garage* (although it wasn't the first episode *Discovery Channel* aired) was because he knew that what I was doing was real. There are people in the industry who have purposely tried to keep me from succeeding. Jesse has never done anything like that. When I see someone who has ill will toward me for whatever reason, I try to straighten it out. But sometimes there isn't much you can do. People just do shitty things sometimes. I figure the best revenge for me is to just do my best work and succeed in spite of the things they do to prevent that from happening. That's part of the reason I did the episode of *Monster Garage*. The show was getting pretty far from building choppers, but it was a way to show people that I was succeeding.

Willie G. and Harley-Davidson

I LIKE Willie G., but I don't like the way Harley does business. Willie G. is a super nice guy, but Harley is a real stuffy, conservative company. Harley uses so much low-quality imported stuff. It's kind of amazing they would do that.

If Harley-Davidson had its way, I wouldn't be in business. Harley doesn't like it when customizers build choppers from their bikes. I don't understand why they feel this way. The way I look at it, the custom bike builders influence all Harley's shit. By the time Harley started building stroked 80-inch engines people had been building stroked engines for years. A custom builder built the first Softail, and when Harley built it's first custom—the Super Glide—people had been customizing Harleys for decades.

The custom builders and Harley help each other. Competition facilitates sales and development. I think Harley forgets that. The aftermarket and custom bike builders might cost them millions in the short term but it makes them billions in the long run.

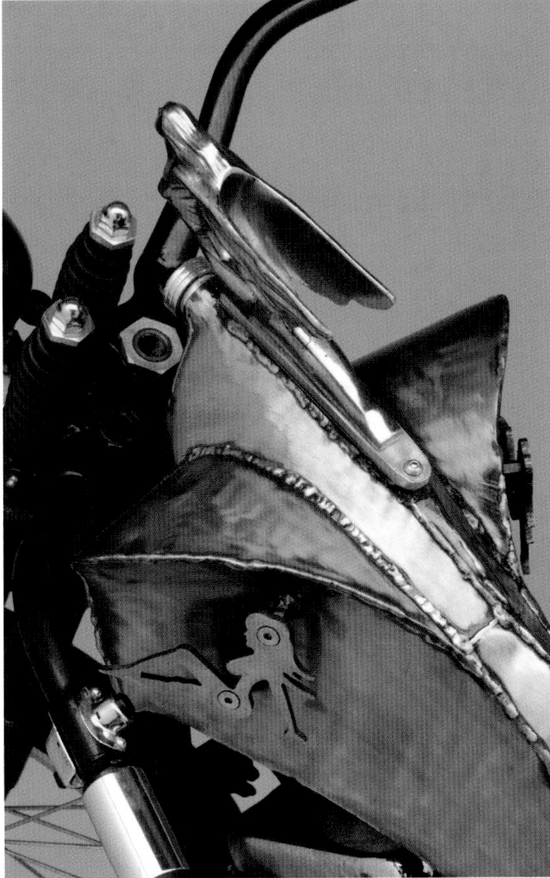

Danny Lyon and Bobbers

I LOVE OLDER HARLEYS. Evo's are great machines, but I think the bikes Harley built prior to that era are the coolest. I have two 1948 bobbers, two 1949 bobbers, and several other 1950s-era bobbers that I've owned for quite some time. They are my favorite bikes. I love bobbers because of Danny Lyon. There is a 1966 Danny Lyon photograph of a Louisville Outlaw crossing the Louisville Bridge on a Panhead bobber. He is wearing his club colors, and he's looking over his right shoulder at something out of frame. His pompadour haircut and long, wide sideburns give away the era in which the photo was taken. The bike's fenders are chrome plated Brit parts, and the rider has a Spanish Conquistador helmet resting atop the headlight. From the first time I saw that photograph, I knew the style was timeless.

My 1950 Panhead was a bobber-style custom when I bought it. Later, when some kids ran me over with their car, we raked it out chopper-like and put a 10 1/2-inch over springer on it. I'd always wanted another bobber, and I got SweetMaryJane in 1998. MaryJane was a 1952 Panhead that I got from my friend Buddy. Buddy's life ended at his own hands, and I rode MaryJane for a couple of years after that tragic event.

Claudia fell off the back of MaryJane once, at a speed of about sixty-five miles per hour. I don't think anyone in Milwaukee ever intended that little Panhead to find itself two feet off the ground at that speed, and it surprised us all when I put us there.

My late friend George loved MaryJane, and used to borrow her all the time. She became his, until someone took his life. Booster has her now, and I think he's crazy for wanting MaryJane. She's a good bike with a bad track record. I'm the only person I know who has ridden and owned that crazy old Pan and is still alive to tell about it. George was riding MaryJane in Michael Lichter's famous photograph "The One and Only," taken near Bear Butte in Sturgis.

My two two-wheeled loves now—the Helle'sBelle (1948) and LeBigMack (1949)—are both bobbers. Both are in original H-D frames with drum brakes. Helle'sBelle is guided by her original springer and LeBigMack uses a HydraGlide front fork. Helle'sBelle got me from Kansas City to Las Vegas, Vegas to Laughlin (I was riding Helle'sBelle when I got arrested), and from Laughlin to Los Angeles with no mechanical problems and no tools. She may be the best bike I've ever ridden. LeBigMack gets her name from the movie *Pulp Fiction*.

My buddy Alex's dad used to drive a Mack truck for a living, and he gave me the Mack dog emblem off that truck. The dog sits proudly between the 1954 fatbob gas tanks, on a dash I made especially for him. That little die-cast bulldog's road days aren't over yet.

I pieced both bikes together from used vintage parts, though they were fairly complete when I got them. What I couldn't find, I made. When I look at these bikes, I feel like I've made it back to my roots, finally. Arlen Ness saw Hell'sBelle on the set of *Big*, and said that it "really brings back a lot of memories." I feel the same way, and it gave me a warm feeling to have him say that to me. I think bobbers are going to be the predominant style in the next few years. They are what you will see me riding.

Thanks, Danny Lyon.

chapter FOUR

Babes, Beer Drinkers, and Hell Raisers

George and Daisy on George's Blue Shovel.

TO SOME degree the people around us shape our lives. I know that's the case with me. Everything I am is a result of the way my parents raised me. I wouldn't ride a chopper if it hadn't been for Warren's influence. I've been really lucky to have some great people in my life. Sometimes it hasn't always worked out the way I'd planned, but I am still grateful for those people having been a part of my life.

There's a pattern with me and women that is as predictable as the tide. We start getting close and I tell them how important the business is to me. Women with kids always say their kids come first. Well, my shop, my customers, and the bikes I build are sort of like my kids, and they come first. When I go to work or to an event, I'm selling my products, my creations. I'm mack mack mack busy. When the women I'm with see this for the first time they get mad because they think I'm ignoring them. They think they are seeing a different person, even though I warned them it was going to be like that. I think they believe they can change me. I don't believe they can.

Myrtle Beach, 2003.

There's a pattern with me and women that is as predictable as the tide.

Shots always taste better
when you drink them from some
hottie's belly button.

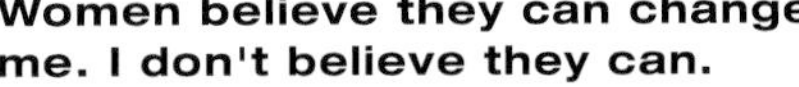
Women believe they can change
me. I don't believe they can.

Claudia

WHEN I MET CLAUDIA, I was hooked on her. I loved her simplicity, her family. She doesn't understand me, and that's our problem. I have tried, with all the strength inside of me, to change that. But I can't. Splitting with her was the hardest thing I've ever had to do. It was also the biggest lift of burden in my life. I would not be where I am today if I had remained with her. That is not negativity toward her; it is negativity toward our relationship. I am outgoing, adventurous, and spontaneous. Claudia was, during our relationship, very conservative and withdrawn. For some couples that works. It didn't for us.

I told her that I was in love with her for the first time one night sitting on my parents' couch. She didn't respond—only looked at me. She didn't feel the same way. I wonder to this day if she knows what that

Splitting with Claudia was the hardest thing I ever had to do.

Dave Nichols, Claudia, and I at the Biker's Ball in Daytona, 2002.

was all about. I have tried to talk to her about it on many occasions, but never got through to her. She was 19; I was 23. She didn't understand me then, and ten years later she still doesn't. I know she wishes she does, and so do I.

Claudia didn't understand when I worked until midnight at the shop. I'd tell her that at least I was working. I wasn't out hitting some chick all night long, but she was jealous of the work, like it was my mistress. I would think a woman, though she wanted her man at home by her side, would be proud that he was that hard-working and dedicated, that he was someone who would be able to support her no matter what, simply because of his work ethic. Forget talent—I would be able to succeed at any trade because of my ability to understand it and learn it, and because I am willing to work as hard as necessary to get what I want. That's the frustrating thing, that no matter how hard I worked at having Claudia, I never really succeeded. Nobody else did either, but I was in the same category with all the rest.

I met her while when she was in college and I waited for her while she was off at graduate school. I'd try to explain that what I was doing with the business—working at the shop and building motorcycles—was my graduate school but she didn't seem to understand. I felt like I'd sacrificed our togetherness so she could have what she wanted, but that she wasn't willing to reciprocate later when I needed it. It hurt.

My life is so crazy, Claudia couldn't tolerate it. There's probably no woman who could.

Claudia and I were together for eight years.

Claudia and I were together for more than eight years. It was heartbreaking when we broke up, but I had to do it. We both thought we were going to get married, have kids. She couldn't give me what I needed, and I wasn't giving her what she needed. We were eating each other alive from the inside out. It looked great on the outside, but my close friends and family knew what it was doing to me.

Claudia's family was really hurt, partly because she didn't let them in on what was happening between us. I think she figured we'd work it out. Had she handed me the answer, we probably could have. I still haven't seen it from her, and I don't have it. I'm sure I am a lot of work to keep down. My life is so crazy that no woman probably could.

I still love Claudia. My love for her is not the intense love that it once was, though. I love her like someone loves his sister. She was seeing some jerk after we broke up and he was

Claudia and I in better times, riding Devil-in-a-Red-Dress in South Dakota.

talking trash about her. I heard him doing it in a bar near my house. I told him he was out of line and he quit. I told Claudia I'd fuck him up, like anyone with any balls would do for their sister, but she didn't want me to do that. I didn't want to have to do it, but I was willing to.

I used to tell Claudia that men and women are different. I'm not saying one is better than the other—I'm just saying they're different. I never expected her to be like me; I just wanted her to understand that I see life from a very different plane than she does. Women can build choppers. They have better finger dexterity then men. I know women who can kick my ass in pool. I know women who can kick my ass in basketball. I know women who can run marathons. I can't run a marathon. I'm getting ready to teach a woman to fabricate custom motorcycles. I intend to make her better than me, at least in skill and craftsmanship. But I don't expect her to understand me, or that I'll understand her. I just hope we accept each other for how different each of us is from the other. Claudia and I weren't able to pull that off.

Niki knew how to fire up a crowd.

Niki

I BROKE UP WITH CLAUDIA AT A crazy time in my life. I was getting ready to start filming the Discovery Channel's *Great Biker Build-Off* television show and my head already wasn't clear. My problems with Claudia weren't conducive to my business or the opportunities that lay ahead.

Claudia and I had been at each other's throats for almost three years. Claudia liked to hide the fact that we had huge differences, but I illuminated the fact out of a sense of preservation. I decided we should split and I was the devil for it. What made it worse was that I met Niki almost immediately. I know that hurt Claudia, but Niki wasn't her replacement. I never expected to find someone who could ever take the spot Claudia held in my life, and that's not what happened.

Niki was a waitress when we met, and I was totally uninterested in her at first. I'd see her where she worked, and "hi" was about as much as either of us would say. She wasn't interested in me, either.

Niki had a boyfriend when we met, but she was unhappy with the relationship and eventually ended it to be with me. She asked a friend where I would be going out one night, and followed me there. Her pick up line was, "Wanna do a shot?" I accepted, and we went back to Nick

Fredella's house. I was afraid to go home, because my deal with Claudia was so fresh. Niki is an extraordinarily beautiful woman, but I fell in love with her because of her personality and charm. If you ever heard her laugh, you'd fully understand. I fell in love with her beauty later on, a rarity for me.

She first told me she loved me while riding behind me on my chopper near Sturgis, South Dakota. We were riding back from Hill City, south of Sturgis. The day was warm and beautiful, and we'd both had plenty of beer and tequila. Niki knows how to party, and she could fire me up. She was doing shots out of other women's belly buttons on the bar at the Mangy Moose Saloon, and the crowd in the bar was loving it. Who doesn't love a hot, blue-eyed blonde sucking booze from another chick's belly button?

The weather deteriorated rapidly, pouring rain and getting extremely cold. The bar got packed, and we tore it up. It became apparent that the weather would not pass through quickly, so we headed from Hill City back to Sturgis. It was cold and hard riding, because we'd left that morning in just jeans and wife-beaters. Friends along the highway gave us a jacket for Niki near Silver City, but I was freezing. The fog was dense,

Riding with Niki in the Black Hills.

and I was struggling against hypothermia and the loss of my visual sense. It was impossible to pull over; we were just too cold. We continued riding, our best option.

We came over a hill on 285, just south of Deadwood, and I looked over my shoulder at Niki and told her we were only about fifteen minutes from town. She told me she loved me, then retracted her statement. She said, "I mean . . . I more than like you." That fucked me up, especially after what had happened with Claudia years before. I didn't say anything, pretended to not hear her, and just kept riding.

We reached Jose's house in Lead, but no one was home. I broke into the house, because we wouldn't have been able to survive that cold, dark night. We drank their beer, talked on the couch. Niki wouldn't fess up to what she'd said on the bike, but I wanted her to come clean. She eventually did, and that has been the pattern for our relationship.

Niki simply never trusted me, and that eventually ended our relationship. No woman has told me she loved me since, except for my mother and one girl I dated. I believe my mother but I'm not so sure about the girl. I wonder if I'll ever hear it again. I know Niki and Claudia both love me, and I love them both back. If I could have them both, I would be the happiest man alive. I doubt that will ever happen, having them both I mean. I continue to work on the other part.

In the end I don't think things worked out between me and Nikki because she never really trusted me.

You meet the nicest girls at strip clubs.

A Bad Reputation

I'VE DATED quite a few women since Niki and I broke up. It has been a strangely interesting time. I could write a book just about that. I don't consider myself famous, just very recognizable. But women see it quite differently, especially if we're spending time together in any manner beyond pure friendship. Most of them know of me before they try to get to know me. What they have already heard has preprogrammed what they will think of me. Anyone who really knows me will tell you that I am down to earth and very humble. But that's not the rap I've got.

Something I've discovered is that many women are drawn to me because of the attention it brings them. Admittedly, I'm not the best looking guy in the world. I know why so many women come around—no one needs to tell me. Some have gotten so caught up in the circus that surrounds me that they think they are the reason for the attention. When they lose that, it is incomprehensible to them. The fact is, I refuse to tolerate disrespect and other bullshit from a woman or any other person.

Dumb men often allow beautiful women to behave poorly. I'm an understanding guy, but I have a threshold for what is acceptable. If that threshold is crossed, I move on. Women hate that about me. It has gotten me the reputation of having been with a lot of women, which, I guess, I have. That reputation is viewed as bad by the women I meet. They all bring it up. I quell the issue by asking them if they suggest I stay with a woman who doesn't understand respect, personal integrity, and honesty. Many don't understand the argument, but they end up next to me anyhow.

I was on a date with a great girl recently, and one of my friends commented in her presence that it was the first time he'd seen me with the same girl twice. She took it as a compliment, as she should have. To have someone appreciate me for who and what I am is a rare find anymore. I can't control how other people perceive me. I can only control what fuels their perceptions.

I'm not dating anyone right now, but I don't seem to spend a lot of time alone.

Whether he's at the shop or partying at Daytona, Nick's a complete madman.

Speeding at Daytona with Nick and George

DURING Daytona Beach Bike Week 2002, Nick Fredella and I were riding from Main Street back to our motel in Ormond, both full of beer and whiskey. Nick was being Nick, riding like a madman in the lane of oncoming traffic. I think he started in on the Budweisers at nine that morning. He rode my 1963 Panhead chopper, the only other person to ever ride it besides me. The Pan was having electrical problems; the generator gear broke. It had quit charging the battery and the lights were going dim. We stopped on Beach Street to disconnect the lights because Ormond was a long ride from where we were and battery voltage was low.

Nick's fangs are real.

A female patrol officer had seen us riding and whipped a U-turn because Nick's lights were so dim. She was cool with our explanation and sent us off with a warning for Nick. The same officer pulled us over again on Atlantic Avenue in Ormond. She followed us into the motel parking lot and called for a backup car. Nick and I are no picnic together, especially when we're loaded. Nick was having fun with the lady officer, and I was having fun watching it all.

The Panhead was registered to me so I had to produce the paperwork to the officer. She was as nervous as a whore in church and her young male companion knew he had his hands full. Nick was drunkenly explaining himself to the police for the second time in an hour as I stood back and they checked our licenses and papers.

I deal with the law frequently and I am not intimidated. Nick is worse than me, and George was worse than Nick. George was a drug dealer for life, a biker for life, and happy to be both. He got out of bed every morning and said, "I'm gonna be the best goddamn drug dealer this world has ever seen." George used to drive cocaine all over the state of Florida, and I'm not talking about gram bags.

Nick and George fooling around at Daytona in 2002.

For some ungodly reason, George walked out of his motel room at what can only be called the critical moment. That, in and of itself, would have been trouble enough, but it was the bag of crystal meth he had that really worried me. I would venture to say, without fear of exaggeration, that there was at least an ounce of crank in that bag. He had also dumped a fat rail out on the carpal side of his hand, which he was ready to introduce into his metabolism.

He was pretty fucked up, and the sight of the cops was not what he wanted. The two officers had their backs to George, and astonishingly were not too concerned with his presence. They surely didn't know his condition, as they acknowledged him with an over-the-shoulder glance. Nick and I had their attention, but they didn't have mine. I was freaking on George and his fix. He'd just gotten off paper from the state of Florida and he didn't need another narco beef.

Nick didn't see it at the time, mainly because he was rapping his way out of a possible DUI arrest, but I watched George snuff that rail of speed and dump another onto his hand. He was six feet from these cops, but a million miles away in his head. I was truly expecting him to offer a bump to the cops. Thankfully he didn't, but he did snort another hit, put the bag of speed away, and try to lay lines of sweetness on the female cop. She wasn't impressed, but she hadn't seen what I had seen.

George and a couple of friends he met one night.

Camping with George

A FEW YEARS AGO we were all staying out at Buffalo Chip Campground for the Sturgis Rally. We'd been out at Sundance, Wyoming, all day, drinking whiskey in the Dime Horseshoe Bar and doing burnouts in the street. The Wyoming State police eventually asked us to leave their fine state, and escorted us to the South Dakota border.

We rode on to Buffalo Chip, where a huge concert was under way in the basin. We all got pretty lit, and George was on fire. After the bands rolled up their equipment, we were all ready to head back up the hill to the campsite. George was too drunk to start SweetMaryJane, so I stepped in to kick her through for him. People panicked, asking, "You're not going to let him ride that, are you?"

"Fuck yeah," I said. "He rides like this all the time." I fired the Pan up and helped George get on. He wobbled about twenty feet and fell over in the dirt. I helped him pick the bike up, and fired it again. People

George and another new friend.

Firing up the pipes on the MoneyShot bike at Daytona.

were trying to step in and intervene so me, Joey Fantastic, and George threatened violence on them all. George made it another twenty feet or so, and fell over again. The third time we got him started, he made it all the way to the foot bridge over the stream that separates the basin from the campsites. That's where the real trouble started.

George crashed into the footbridge and fell over. He wouldn't let anyone help him until Fantastic and I arrived. He was all bloody with his hair covering his face and mumbling some unknown rhetoric, but it was clear that he wanted the bike restarted immediately. I kicked it for him again, and prayed he would make it over the bridge and up the hill. He did make it over the bridge and, surprisingly, up the hill. The hill is tough to navigate, because it hooks around to the right pretty hard, the gravel is very loose, and it is bordered on either side by campsites. MaryJane has suicide shift and no front brakes. He had a few near misses with tents on

Michael Lichter's "The One and Only."

the way up, but he made it past. Claudia and I walked up to our campsite, but George and MaryJane weren't there. I was worried that George had circled around and gone back to the basin-or worse, decided to get on the valley road and ride back into town.

Just then we heard some yelling from a campsite below us on the hill and we knew George had to have some involvement. We walked down and there he was, in all his glory. George ran his bike into some sleeping couple's igloo-shaped tent. He and the bike fell over on top of the tent, pulling its stakes up while they were still inside. His headlight was hanging out of its bucket, by the wires. George had undone his pants to take a leak, but passed out drunk before his body was able to perform that function.

The people sleeping in the tent quietly asked us, "Does this man belong to you?"

I answered, "Yes, he does."

"Well, would it be too much to ask for you to get him the fuck off our tent?"

Being the diplomat, I said, "If you can't be nice about it, I'll just leave him here." The guy's attitude changed quickly, and I started to drag George off. He woke up, and tried to pick up the guy's girl. That's my boy.

In Lichter's photograph, MaryJane has a price sticker on the headlight. That's because the photograph was taken the day after George ran his bike into those people's tent. I had to ride into Sturgis and get him another bulb from the parts store.

There's a story behind that price tag on George's headlight.

Warren and Georgie in George's Caddy.

Author Photo

George's Blue Shovel

ONE NIGHT, a bunch of us were drinking hard at a bar. George was completely fucked up. We were drinking Crown Royal, Jose Cuervo, and Corona. He didn't know what Corona meant in English so I explained it. He thought I was so smart for knowing that. Afterwards he called Crown Royal "Corona Royal." He would fuck up pronunciation of words a lot, and his friends all loved it. It made him seem dumb sometimes, but he was one of the smartest people I've ever known.

One night Big John, president of the Warlocks Motorcycle Club, rode George's Shovelhead home because George had drunk way too much and smoked too much reefer. We got back to George's garage and drank a bunch more. Big John is huge, and made that Shovel look small. George was proud that night to have John ride his bike. George loved John, and a lot of other one percenters. He probably would have become one someday, had time not run out on him.

We used to do this thing when we surfed, where we would howl like the wrestler Rick Flair. I hipped George to it one time, and we never quit. He'd do it riding, when he met a hottie, whenever. I like to do it when I walk into a bar, like he used to. People turn around and want to know what the hell all the noise is about. If you think you'll ever turn around and see George, it's not going to happen. George was murdered by his girlfriend Jodie.

The Death of George

I WALKED THROUGH George's front yard with the Sheriff's detectives as Jodie was sitting handcuffed in the rear of a patrol car. She glared at me as I walked by, like I didn't belong. She makes excuses, but I don't understand why she just didn't leave George. It doesn't matter; we will never speak again. She is the only human that I truly hate. She made a huge mistake.

George loved her. Shortly before he died he told me things I doubt he ever told another human. Anyone who thinks they knew him hasn't heard what I have. It was a shame what that girl did to his life, and I mean before she took it. My relationship with George had come full circle; man, he was asking *me* for help. I feel fortunate to have been in a situation to help him because I was the last person to be able to do so. George was always generous, and it felt good to help him instead of take his help. That's what he was used to. He had one of the strongest characters a person can have. I'm attracted to that shit.

I've never felt so helpless as I did when Jodie murdered George. Her daughters, through all they have seen, are a delight. I pray those girls get the right guidance and have a good life. Jodie is a worthless life to me.

I'd take it if I could, but I don't like waiting in line. In my adult life, I can only recall crying three times. Once was with Claudia—we cried together. Good times. Once, I'm not going into. And I cried at George's funeral.

I pulled a big-ass wheelie in the parking lot of the funeral home when we arrived to see him off. I wish he would have jumped up out of the casket and screamed, but he didn't. He just lay there, lifeless. I was riding Blue, the Shovelhead chopper I had built for him. It won an award at *Easyriders* magazine's national invitational bike show in Columbus, Ohio in 2001. We all love to do the *Easyriders* shows, and George was the life of the party at every one. The *Easyriders* people loved having George around, and graced their October 2002 cover with his bike. George was extremely proud to have won that bike show and to have made that magazine cover. He told me once that those might have been the best moments of his life. *Easyriders* has done him right since his death, and doing that wheelie was just one of the ways I have tried to do the same.

I bought his truck from his family after his death, and think about this next story every time I drive it. One day I called to tell him

the waves were good, and he soon pulled up to my house to go surfing—with sixteen kilos in the back seat of his truck. I said, "Bro', what the fuck are you doing? Are you crazy? You can't leave sixteen kilos of coke in your truck while we surf."

I was called as a witness in Jodie's trial in the spring of 2004. It was hard to do, because I have tried to put the details and negativity surrounding George's death behind me. However, I was glad to do it because I would like to see Jodie get what she deserves. Her brother, who used to be cool with me and to me, shot me a couple of shitty stares. I think he was angry that I was there to tell the truth about what happened. Her defense was that she felt threatened by George. Jodie's lawyer's approach was to paint a dirty picture of George and his friends for the jurors. I don't know what difference it makes if all of a person's friends are drug dealers, felons, bikers, tattoo artists, or potheads, but Jodie's lawyer seemed to think it was a legitimate reason for his client to have killed our friend.

I had just pulled into Las Vegas from Kansas City when I heard that Jodie was acquitted of the murder charges in George's death. I was stunned. Claudia text-messaged me and I think it took a few hours to really take hold. Our friend Diamond Dave just left to spend the next three years of his life in a federal prison in Texas for owning a gun that has never been fired, and Jodie was able to walk away after a year in jail awaiting trial for shooting our friend four times. She was acquitted of murder and I got arrested for running out of gas.

I value my one-percenter friends who I've known since before this whole thing blew up. They know what I'm going through.

Me and Tony Pierce, one percenter, Main Street, Sturgis.

Loneliness

I WAS ASKED RECENTLY if it's lonely to be where I am sometimes. The answer didn't immediately pop into my mind. When you start getting famous you end up getting a little isolated. That can lead to huge loneliness. The loneliness isn't the physical kind, where I can't get a date, and it doesn't come from being alone. I've been with people who I can't wait to get away from. To truly consider someone a friend, I think there has to be some mutual understanding of who each person is. This goes for men and women. Most people just don't understand what it is like to not be able to walk down the street, eat at a restaurant, or kiss your girl in public without being interrupted by someone. My time isn't fully mine anymore, and that sometimes causes people to think I have changed as a person. I have not, but it has caused me turmoil in my relationships with both sexes.

Even though I'm always with a lot of people, sometimes the life I lead is kind of isolating.

There's not a lot I can do about the situation. People are always around me, but they don't understand what I'm going through. It's real hard because most people haven't experienced what this is like. I used to wonder why movie stars marry movie stars and rock stars marry rock stars. Now I understand. It's because they know what the other one is going through. Most people have no comprehension. I've tried not to change as a person, but this has changed my life. I've had to adjust the way I live.

My friends who knew me before, like Smitty, they understand. Smitty's hardcore, an old-school biker who lives the lifestyle. He's been riding Harleys since 1963 and rebuilds Panheads for a living. He lost an inch of his leg in a motorcycle crash and now he's got tattoos of his X-rays on his leg, complete with all the hardware. You press down on the tattooed screw in his leg and you can feel the real screw underneath. Smitty sees people mobbing me and he gets what I'm going through.

I got myself into this but when I started I had no idea what I was getting myself into. I look at people who decided not to get into a position like this, people like Pat Kennedy, who chose to stay out of the public eye. If I had to do it over again, I really don't know if I'd pick this route or do it like Pat Kennedy.

Michael Licter's "That's Why We're Here."

No matter where I go or what I do, it seems like there's always someone with a bottle of Jack Daniels handy.

chapter FIVE

Big INK

Forming metal the hard way.

PEOPLE THINK I just started building bikes in 2003 when they saw me on television. They think I just fell out of the sky like a lot of the builders who are jumping on the bandwagon now. They have no idea that I've devoted most of my adult life to doing this. People think they can get on TV without putting in the work needed to learn the craft. Some of them do pretty well that way, but I paid my dues to learn how to build choppers. When I started building bikes I never dreamed I'd be on television. Even when Jesse got *Motorcycle Mania* I never thought I'd be there.

With Jesse Jurrens of Legend Air and Kendall Johnson.

Monster Garage

BEFORE the television stuff, people would vaguely recognize me from magazines. They'd say, "Have I seen you somewhere before?" I'd say, "I don't know. Do you rent a lot of porn?" I still use that response, but not as frequently. These days, people approach me everywhere I go and know exactly why they recognize me. I can thank the Discovery Channel for that.

Jesse James invited me to participate in an episode of Original Productions' television show *Monster Garage* on the Discovery Channel. I wasn't sure I wanted to be a part of it. I thought the idea sounded pretty whacked—turning a Mustang into a lawn mower. Claudia didn't want me to do it, but I thought it might be good for the business. We hadn't been getting along for a few years and this helped push us over the edge. I headed to Los Angeles to film the show. We began filming the weekend prior to Thanksgiving in 2001.

One morning after it aired I was on my bike in traffic, waiting for a train to pass near my shop. A bunch of girls in a minivan next to me started screaming my name, and two of them flashed their tits at me. They looked like teenagers, and it seemed illegal, but it was cool, so I encouraged more. That was the moment when I began to understand the power of television.

If it wasn't for exposure in biker magazines like *Easyriders* and *The Horse,* my business wouldn't have blown up as big as it did.

Biker Build-Off

I REMAINED in contact with the folks at Original Productions after doing *Monster Garage*, and let them know that I would be interested in working with them again if they ever considered filming other television shows involving custom motorcycle builders. Original, prior to creating *Monster Garage*, produced the two groundbreaking documentaries about Jesse James and his motorcycles: *Motorcycle Mania I* and *II*. I also let some heavy hitters in the motorcycle industry know about my interest, Including Dave Nichols and Michael Lichter from *Easyriders* magazine. That happened during Daytona Beach Bike Week in March, 2002. Before the end of the month, Dave Nichols called me to tell me that Original had the green light from Discovery to produce *Motorcycle Mania III*,

Me pulling into the parking lot to meet Dave Perewitz for the second Biker Build Off.

Heading out on the road with Dave and his crew.

and that the show was to be about my life, my bikes, and my business. Dave is a known prankster, and though he had never lied to me, I wasn't sure how to take his words. I decided to wait to hear it from either Hugh King or Thom Beers from Original. Their calls came in successively, and I knew my life would never be the same again. I have never been more right about anything.

Original came in with their production crew in April, 2002. I tried to have Choppers Inc. as prepared as possible for what was to come. Claudia still worked for me at the time, and we decided not to broadcast our personal problems to the cameras. Naturally, the pressures of working in front of a film crew under tough time constraints caused our problems to rise to the surface. Original's cameras captured quite a bit of that on film. It caused me great anxiety, wondering how that would play out on television. I was extremely happy and impressed with Original's judgment in not using any of that footage. It would have hurt Claudia and me both, and I bet we would not be friends today if they chose otherwise.

As filming progressed Hugh King informed me that they would be changing the format of the program. He told me that the show would not be *Motorcycle Mania III*, and that it would most likely include a competition of some sort with another builder. Hugh asked me to name some other prominent names in the industry. I suggested Matt Hotch, Russell Mitchell, Paul Yaffe. I didn't suggest Indian Larry because I didn't think he was still building bikes. It turned out that he was just getting back into building bikes after taking some time off. If I had known that, Larry would have been at the top of my list. Most of them, if not all, have since been asked to participate in future episodes of what is now called *The Great Biker Build-Off.*

That first *Biker Build-Off* eventually turned into a competition between myself and Roger Bourget from Phoenix, Arizona. I never thought about Roger Bourget. Not that he wouldn't make a worthy opponent—he's a very capable builder. It's just that he's known more as a manufacturer than a builder. But they picked Roger, and it worked out pretty well.

Prior to being informed that Roger would be my competition, Hugh and I discussed which biker events would make a good a late-summer venue to wrap the show up. Original didn't want to use Sturgis, because they'd used it to wrap up *Motorcycle Mania II* with Jesse. *The Horse* magazine was holding its third annual Horse Smokeout in Salisbury, North Carolina, from June 26 to 28. Logistically, the Smokeout was perfect. I had been involved with *The Horse* practically since its inception, and I had been an avid reader of the magazine's predecessor,

Dave and I taking a break.

Hugh giving Dave and I direction.

Iron Horse, for many years. I suggested the event to Hugh and Original, entirely out of support for the magazine and its event.

The situation that emerged was undeniably advantageous to myself regarding the outcome of that build-off. Simply put, *The Horse* magazine is a hardcore chopper magazine. I was and still am on staff at the magazine, as well as being a continuing advertiser. Its event reflects that and, being more of a high-end production bike builder rather than a custom chopper builder like myself, Roger had no chance with that crowd. Roger is gifted and smart, and he handled it well. He has undoubtedly benefited from participating in that show, regardless of the outcome. He's one guy who deserved widespread recognition and he got it.

We call the bike I built for that show "MissBehavin'". It belongs to my good friend and co-worker, Ruskin. That bike has become extremely famous. People recognize it everywhere we ride it. Ruskin and I have ridden that bike all over this country. It has held up well, but is in need of some fresh paint at the moment.

After filming the first episode, Original Production called us back and asked us to participate in *Biker Build-Off II*. We began filming that show in late February 2003. This time we knew who I'd be building against, the legendary builder and painter Dave Perewitz from Massachusetts. Dave has been a huge inspiration to me, and to even be classed with him was a complete and total honor. His bikes, along with the creations of Arlen Ness, Donnie Smith, and Arlin Fatland were always in the pages and on the covers of the big bike magazines when I became

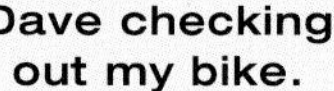

Dave checking out my bike.

interested in all of this. Their ingenuity and workmanship seemed unobtainable to me then, and here I was building against one of them.

Timing was awful for me, but I knew I had to produce. We started filming just prior to Daytona Bike Week, and we were swamped with work and personal issues. RJ Reynolds Tobacco commissioned us to build a bike for their Camel Roadhouse Tour, then one of the most prestigious events in the custom motorcycle world. That bike was due a day prior to Bike Week. We committed to building and donating a custom bike to *Easyriders* magazine for their VQ Biker Ball Charity Auction, also due during Bike Week. We relocated to a new shop and were moving tons of equipment, motorcycles, and parts, a huge undertaking. Niki and I had finally made it to the point where we had to part ways. George had been dead for exactly one month, and Booster, Big Al, Smitty, Joey Fantastic, Nick, and myself had spent most of the time since then helping his family and friends deal with what was left. I was a busy guy, and Original's cameras recognized that clearly.

Dave and I admiring each other's work.

I was told Dave Perewitz was taking the whole thing very seriously, while I decided to mostly blow it off. Originally, I had everything well planned out. I made comprehensive lists of the parts I would need from elsewhere and of the parts I would have to make by hand. I had a list of materials that would need to be ordered. I talked with my crew about how I wanted the show to go down. Roger Bourget was no joke, and Dave is a much more experienced builder than Roger. Collectively, my crew let me down. Not much was ready when Original returned with their cameras to begin filming *The Great Biker Build-Off II*. I was pissed at everyone, and rightly so. Therefore, I blew off *The Great Biker Build-Off II* in a huge way.

I hadn't spent much time thinking about how the bike was going to look. I designed the frame a year prior to actually using it, and it was different than anything I'd ever used. I knew I would have trouble with the gas tank, because of the non-typical configuration of the frame.

What better way to film a motorcycle than from another motorcycle?

Nick cooling down the pipes with some bottled water.

We started filming, and Nick and I put the rolling chassis together including the wheels, tires, frame, front fork, and brakes. We also installed the engine and transmission, and that's where the trouble started. We'd done the easy work, and the difficult part was all that lay ahead.

I began working on the rear fender, and used a thought I'd had for some time. I decided to make the rear fender house the exhaust tips. My metal-forming equipment was located in our new shop, but there was no electric power or air pressure there to run it. I had to form the panels for the exhaust out of pre-existing curves stolen from a conventional rear fender. I was able to make it work, but it took me more time than it should have. I still needed to fabricate the gas tank, and we were virtually out of time. The film crew was ready to fly back to California. I'd wasted a lot of time, and knew it would create pressure during the next filming segment.

When we started filming again, I immediately went to work on the fuel tank. I started forming it, mostly unaware of what it would look like when done. My mind was blank, and I just started forming panels. The tank took shape slowly. I built it out of seventeen panels in total, which meant a lot of seam welding. It took the entirety of our second filming segment to make it. Stress took over a few times, and we went out drinking at night instead of working overtime or resting. Overtime usually means the difference between an eighteen hour day and a twenty hour day when filming a *Biker Build-Off* segment. Rest is almost non-existent. Drinking should be forbidden, but we did it anyhow. Fortunately, my welds were tight, and I found very few leaks in the tank when I pressure tested it.

We sent the frame and gas tank to Joe Richardson's for paint. He'd been expecting the sheet metal a few days earlier, but my indiscretions landed him another rush job. I told him I thought blue would be a good color, but to do whatever he wanted. Joe chose traffic cone orange, which disgusted me. The paint job was perfect and beautiful, but I absolutely hated the color. I was stuck with his choice, but I was soon to find out that that was the least of my problems.

After sending the frame out to be painted, I realized I'd forgotten a major concern: I never addressed how the rear brake was to be fastened to the frame. In all of the commotion going on around me, I simply forgot it. Nick had been busy assembling our VQ Bike, so he wasn't there to back me up like he sometimes is. This was a huge mistake that cost me many later headaches. The final filming segment with Original was only scheduled for two days' time allotted for assembly of the bike. Since the frame had already been painted, welding to it was not an option. Everything in the back end of the bike was a tight fit, and my oversight in the matter cost me an entire day of work in the machine shop creating a way to stop a 130-horsepower, 500-pound motorcycle.

Me examining the charred remnants of my seat after it caught fire on the ride.

Fixing the belt at Magic Touch Customs in Shreveport, Louisiana.

Luckily, I invited Aaron Greene from Paramount Custom Cycles in Reno to ride with us to our destination in Dallas. He arrived early, ready and willing to work to help me finish the bike. While I machined metal trying to fix the brake problem, Nick and Aaron went to work assembling the rest of the parts. They worked around the clock with the help of my friends Bean're, Jose DeMiguel, and Big John. Without their help, I would have called the producers of the show and told them I was out. I was dead tired and out of patience.

We were supposed to meet Perewitz and the film crew in Pensacola, Florida, and ride west from there. I was already a day late when I left, so they decided to ride on without me to a location in Baton Rouge. What most people don't know is that Original Production's film crew completed production at Dave's shop two weeks prior to the date they arrived at my shop. In other words, Dave's bike was done, but he had two weeks to tweak it, ride it, refine it, and make last minute adjustments before it was expected to perform, while I was forced to let my bike sit unfinished until the cameras returned. Then, I was expected to piece it together in two days and hit the road, with no time to even test ride it. Dave had a serious advantage over me, and I say that without complaint. What bothered me then was how some of Dave's friends handled my being late.

Custom hand-formed tanks that hold one or two gallons of gas look great, but they aren't the most practical things for long-distance touring.

Dave invited many of his friends and family to join us on our ride. Most of them were great company to have, and have become my friends also. But a few were assholes, on and off camera. When I didn't arrive on time, one of his friends mentioned on film that I should have ridden a Bourget instead of my own bike. There was nothing wrong with my bike once it was finished. I just wasn't going to ride a bike that wasn't ready. I took the necessary time to finish it. They were waiting on me, but that show wasn't for or about them. It was about me and Dave, and they were only along to suck what little fame they could from the two of us. I heard them talking shit about me again in the hotel lobby after I won the *Build-Off,* but they didn't know I was listening. It's sad to see grown men—successful enough to be able to afford one of Dave Perewitz's great custom motorcycles—make assholes of themselves on television simply by opening their mouths and letting their ego overrun common sense. I'd hate to put on those shoes any morning. Dave acted like a perfect gentleman, and we will always remain friends in my opinion.

Easyriders* editor Dave Nichols announcing me as the winner of the second *Biker Build-Off.

Along the way to Dallas, I broke my final drive belt pulling wheelies. I was showing off for the cameras. A few of Dave's friends bitched about that, too, while others pitched in to help out. We spent the next day in Shreveport at Magic Touch Customs fixing the belt. The owners of the shop and their employees and friends were gracious one percenters, and let us take over their shop. We drank beer and whiskey all day, and fixed our bikes, while Dave and his friends motored on to Dallas. Those people were real bikers helping other bikers out. People like that are rare, and make me keep wanting to do what I do. I wish at least some of the footage Original shot that day would have made it on the Discovery Channel, because those people are really what bikers are all about. They opened their arms to us because we needed help.

Paul Yaffe builds some extremely clean custom bikes and made a worthy competitor for Indian Larry on *Biker Build-Off.*

We rode on to Dallas in the pouring rain—myself, my friend Bean're, Ruskin, Aaron Greene, and a film crew. It rained virtually the whole way to Dallas, and we rode most of the way in the dark. That was some hard riding, and to have someone knock me for doing it was insulting.

We arrived at Rick Fairless' Strokers Bar in Dallas around 10:00 p.m. Friday night. There was a huge crowd anticipating us, and it is fair to say that they drank heavily before we got there. The place was rocking, full of custom bikes and beautiful Texas women—just my style. Choppers, Inc. people like to show off, and we lit the tires up when we pulled in. The path inside the bar was narrow, with bikes lined up on either side. I revved the throttle and dumped my clutch, and I could hear Ruskin doing the same right behind me on MissBehavin.' I liked it, because we were late and didn't care. I figured, let people be mad at us—we'll party so hard with them that they won't be able to remember any of it. We had to make a hard left turn past a row of bikes, and people were crowding the path. I almost ran over one woman.

Over my right shoulder I saw a bright light, and a flash of chrome and red paint as I turned. Ruskin's Mikuni carburetor stuck wide open as he pulled a wheelie, and it caught him off guard. I ducked his handlebars and watched him sail out of control through the crowd. People bailed out of the way. It was unreal. We were tired from riding all day, and here goes Ruskin like a madman through the crowd. I thought he was showing off, but he had no choice. Instead of taking the left turn I did, MissBehavin' took him right into the cement wall at the rear of Strokers. I think MissBehavin' took out six bikes that night.

Getting some tips from Indian Larry.

All of the owners were real cool about it except for one. He wouldn't let it go, even after we promised to pay for the damage (we did). I thought about dropping him, but he looked old enough to have possibly been a Vietnam vet, so I passed on him. What an entrance.

We partied all night at Strokers, and did the *Easyriders* Bike Show the next morning. The show rocked, and we had a great time. Dallas received us well. During the show, Discovery had ballot boxes in which each attendee was supposed to cast their vote for either Dave or myself to determine the winner of the *Biker Build-Off.* Everyone seemed to love my bike, and it looked like I would win the voting. I personally watched several of Dave's friends repeatedly go

Larry with Kendall Johnson and Jesse Jurrens.

Larry taking one of Jesse Jurrens' bikes out for a shakedown cruise.

back to his ballot box and stuff handfuls of votes in for him. There was a slip-up at the show, and people were able to take however many voting slips they wanted. A couple of my guys were infuriated when they saw this and they came to me. I told them to let it fly, mainly out of concern for Dave. I didn't think he was behind it or aware of it, and I didn't want it to seem that way. I'd rather lose than disrespect him like that. *Easyriders'* people caught wind of this, and saw it for themselves. They, too, were furious. I thank them for standing up and doing the right thing in a tricky situation. Nobody likes a liar or a cheater.

Those who did this know who they are were if any of them ever to try to deny it happened, I won't be gracious enough again to omit their names as I have here. They can thank Beau Allen Pacheco's *American Rider* article for me bringing this up. I was willing to let it lie, but Beau suggested quite vigorously that it was my guys who were stuffing the ballot box in my favor. Why he would write that I don't know, and I think he personally owes me an explanation. I doubt I'll ever get it, so he'll have to exist without my respect. I'd rather it be otherwise, but I believe there is always the opportunity to make things right.

Larry: "Either you need a main jet that's this much smaller..."

"...or a tittie that's this much bigger."

Larry watching Nick work.

I ended up winning *Great Biker Build-Off II*, and Dave took it like a gentleman. I didn't care that I won; I was just happy to have been able to do the show. People love that program, and I'm proud to have been a part of it.

The most memorable moment in the show was when my pants and jacket caught on fire. I knew the seat would get very hot initially, and intended to solve that problem before we left for Dallas. Time was not on my side, however, and we left without addressing the situation. I have since solved the problem, with the help of a company called Aspen Aerotech. They saw me on TV, and sent me a sheet of insulation that rejects the heat under the seat. It is much more pleasant to ride now.

During the course of filming *Biker Build-Off II*, I had Paul Cox make a seat for my bike. Paul made the seat for MissBehavin' also. While we were filming *Biker Build-Off II*, Hugh King from Original Productions asked me who would be a good candidate for another *Build-Off* program. I suggested Indian Larry from Brooklyn, who happens to share shop space with Paul Cox. When Paul offered to give me my seat for free, I said, "Fuck that—if you're not going to let me pay you, then let me fly you and Larry down here to Florida to meet the Discovery People and do this on TV." Paul's act of generosity paid off, because Indian Larry ended up being on the *Biker Build-Off III* with Paul Yaffe and Biker *Build-Off IV* with me.

Filming the fourth *Build-Off* show was probably the most fun I've ever had in my shop. I learned to have faith in no one but myself, and I was fully prepared for it. I built my bike—WholeLottaRosie—with very little flash. I relinquished the idea of competing with Larry. I didn't care about winning or losing. At that point, I had already accomplished everything I'd ever set as a goal for myself in my industry. Being on TV was just an added bonus, and winning didn't even matter. I built the kind of bike I always wanted. I love rigid-framed springers with generator engines and no electric start. I didn't chrome the engine or frame. The paint is black, with no graphics or flames. The bike said what I wanted it to: "I don't have to prove anything to anyone anymore."

Larry and Nick chilling in the shop.

If you ever see Nick without a beer, it's probably not Nick.

I did all of the fab work on WholeLottaRosie alone, except for the exhaust pipes. Nick did some of that with me. I learned a lot about myself building that bike. I built it as a remembrance of my friend George, and I thought about him while I built it. I named the bike after the AC/DC song. Listen to the words and look at that bike. The opening lines fit that bike perfectly, and the guitar riffs sound like what was going through my mind when I built it.

I was supposed to be the one with the advantage during this filming, because my bike would have been done two weeks prior to Larry's last filming segment. Everything was going smoothly for me, and I put myself on cruise control versus working frantically against the clock. Accurate Engineering rebuilt a new S&S generator Shovel engine that Custom Chrome gave me for Rosie, but I added a twist. I used a set of dual-carb Shovelhead heads that had been George's on the bike. The set is two rear heads, with the head for the front cylinder rotated backwards. It is an old racing trick from the 1960s, and I had to have it on my new baby.

I had the bike finished, minus a few parts I couldn't make without the engine. Berry and his guys drove the engine down from Alabama, and we installed it in the bike. I needed the engine to make the top motor-mount, exhaust pipes, air cleaners, and primary drive. The chain drive primary is something I've wanted to do for years. It consists of three double-row H-D primary chains and a clutch assembly I made from three H-D stock clutch assemblies. It is dangerous as hell, but looks cool and eats denim. My problems began when I finally got everything together. I expected to receive a running, tuned, ready-to-go engine for the bike. Discovery's cameras were on hand when I first tried to start it. I can kick start any bike. I have kick started bikes with 131-ci engines before. But the 103-inch Shovel didn't respond to my leg at all. It wasn't even trying to run.

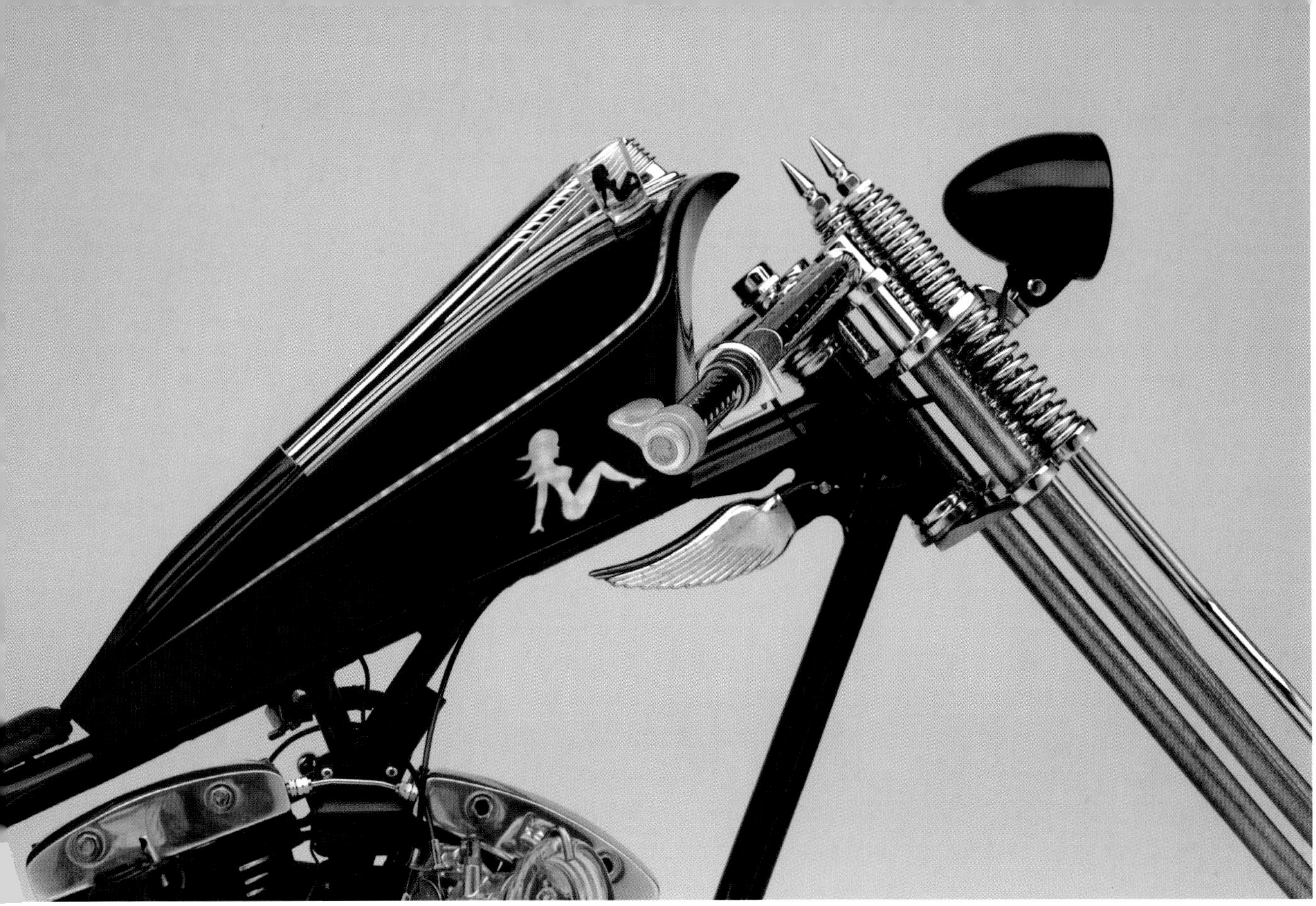

I called Berry, and he said that it had run on the stand in his shop for a while. I'm an experienced mechanic, and I knew something was wrong when I first saw the engine. DaVinci Carburetors donated the two S&S Shorty G model carburetors that were on the bike. I mentioned to Berry that the engine was over carbureted with two Gs on it—I thought it should have two E-models. I would expect one G-model to be enough to fuel 103 inches. DaVinci bores their carbs out and does a lot of tricks to make them perform better than S&S intends them to. I knew two worked Gs would be trouble, but I took their word that they would work.

When I got nowhere, I called Berry and told him the bike was either out of time, not producing spark, over carbureted, or any combination of the three. I decided to call before checking anything myself, because I didn't want to step on anyone's toes. I really didn't want to mess with it, either. Berry insured me that those were the carbs DaVinci recommended. I don't blame Berry or DaVinci for the screw up. It is my own

fault. I messed up big by not trusting my own instincts. Berry ran the engine on his bench at Accurate, but they started it with an electric starter. The electric starter was able to roll the engine over at a higher speed than my leg can kick. The magneto ignition produced spark at that speed, but not at the lower rpm I was kicking at. They also ran it at around 1000 rpm, but must have never brought it down to idle speed. Had I known those two facts, my life would be much different today. That's an amazing thing to think about.

I pulled the magneto and put an electronic ignition in the bike, and it began to respond. It was still grossly over carbureted, and I knew it. I put the smallest jets in the carburetors that exist, and it was still swallowing too much fuel. I kicked and kicked that bike for ten days straight

After an incredible amount of trouble, we finally made it into Sturgis for the fourth *Biker Build-Off.*

all day—one thing people didn't see on television. I was worn out and frustrated, and Original Productions was up my ass about it. I was supposed to leave for St. Louis to meet up with Indian Larry and his crew, but the bike wasn't ready on account of the engine. I called Larry and told him I was having major trouble, and he was way cool about it. Original's producers told me they needed me and the bike in Missouri, that their crew was waiting, and that I was costing them money. I put it to them like I do with everybody. I told them that I wasn't riding on Interstate 70 with an underpowered, mistuned bike. They told me to get it to St. Louis, and we could work the problems out there. Those two days in St. Louis turned out to be the meat and potatoes of that show.

I was really frustrated, and my right leg was whipped. The day we were getting ready to leave for St. Louis, I decided to take the bike for a few test rides. It ran like hell, but I wanted to at least get used to it a little before going on camera and across the country. I went to kick start it, and the transmission main shaft broke in half as I went through it. Anyone who has ever freewheeled a worn-out four-speed kick starter knows how much this hurts. If you don't know, you're lucky. I hyper-extended my knee, and was raging mad. I didn't feel like working anymore, and I knew it would be a full day's work to replace that main shaft. Nick saw my frustration and jumped on the job for me. He saved my ass. My knee was throbbing, and I almost kicked that bike over on it's side. I was going to call Original and tell them to forget me, and I damn near did. That would have been a mistake. Nick calmed me down and solved one of my problems for me. Others were waiting around the corner.

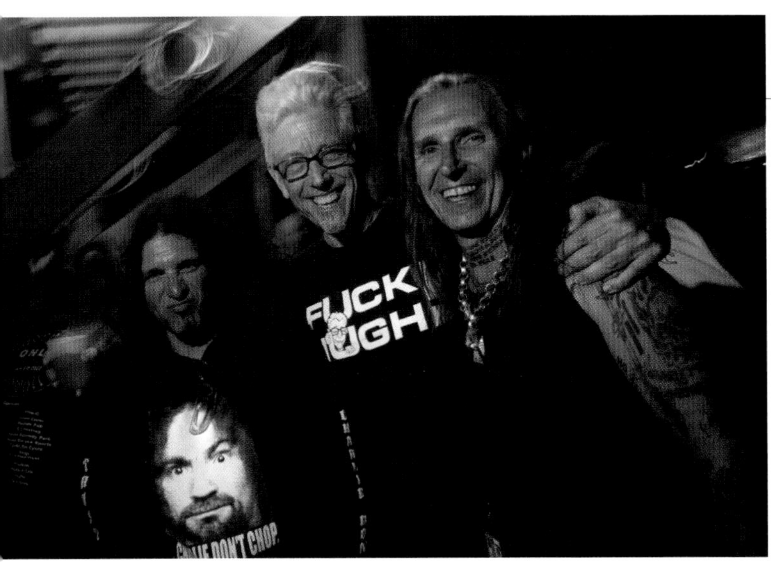

Original Production's Hugh King with Larry and I.

Hugh King announcing Larry as the winner of the fourth *Biker Build-Off.*

I flew into St. Louis, and had a great day with Larry, his guys, and the Original Productions crew. We were waiting on my truck to arrive with the *Build-Off* bike. Nick called me from Tennessee with bad news. The truck's transmission overheated and pumped all of its fluid onto the highway. We had a 40-foot trailer behind it with $450,000 worth of custom motorcycles inside, and leaving it on the highway was not an option. They had to get the truck and trailer towed to a dealership, and it was already late afternoon. I pissed the film crew off again, even though I was a victim of the very same circumstances myself.

Nick arrived late that night with my bike. Original immediately wanted to film, and I wanted to rest and wait until morning. I lost. We headed to a paint shop in town called Liquid Illusions, where Larry and I got to see each other's bikes for the first time. Larry's bike was impressive, and I knew the moment I saw it that he would most-likely become the winner of that build-off. I didn't care; I just needed a vacation and wanted to ride to Sturgis. Larry is always cool, and he put in a great effort to help me get my Shovel running. MidUSA Motorcycle Parts is located right there in St. Louis, and they hooked me up with two smaller S&S Super E carburetors. It took some modifying to install them on the big intakes, but the bike ran considerably better right away. My instincts had been correct, and I wish I had followed them from the beginning.
We changed the fuel metering jets down to the smallest possible size, and the bike ran better yet. It was still not perfectly tuned, and that worried me. We would be climbing several thousand feet in altitude, and that would make an over-carbureted situation worse. I wanted more time to tune but Original's producer, Hugh King, told me it was time to go or go home.

We rode on through Missouri and Kansas, into Nebraska, and up through South Dakota on Route 285. We were down south of Custer, coming around a bend in the road, when we encountered a herd of buffalo crossing the highway. They had some calves with them, and the bulls were hostile. They didn't like the sound of our engines, and our headlights had them spooked. Two of them started toward us, and we were seriously thinking we were going to be charged. I decided to bail off my bike and when I did, I rolled downhill in their direction. That scared them off, and they moved away down the hill.

About a mile down the road, we saw the silhouette of a buffalo on the left-hand side of the road. Larry and I both tapped our brakes, until we realized it was a state park sign silhouetted to look like a buffalo. Larry was in front and to the right of me. It was a good thing we slowed down momentarily, because

Larry with the trophy, just before we cut it in half.

a deer crossed the road between us at full trot. I was only about five feet off Larry's rear tire, leaving very little room between our bikes for the deer to pass. Had we not hit our brakes when we saw that state park sign, one of us would have collided with that deer. I had to tell Larry about it. He never saw it. It freaked me out. Former *Easyriders* editor Keith Ball hit a deer the year before in Wyoming, on his way to Sturgis. I didn't want it to be my turn.

In Sturgis, we had a great time with the *Build-Off* fans and voters. People really seemed to enjoy the bikes and our presence. My crew and Larry's all got along great, and neither side cared how the event would turn out. I'd been thinking while riding through Nebraska, that no one should win or lose. I decided that if we won I would cut the trophy in half, and give half to Larry. I didn't mention it to anyone, though. I really thought Larry would win and, at last, we would be able to go home and rest for a while.

I planned to go to the Home Depot in Rapid City and buy an angle grinder with a big cutting wheel, like we use to cut metal in the shop. I got pretty swamped during the week and forgot to do it. Toward the end of the last day, before the ballots were counted, I sent Ruskin over to my friend PeeWee's shop across Main Street from the Roadhouse, where we were set up. I told him to borrow a grinder with a cutting wheel, but not to tell anyone what it was for. I didn't even want my crew knowing what I had planned, because I didn't want it to seem like we thought we were going to win. Just prior to having the winner announced, and while we were on stage, I pulled Larry toward me and told him that I intended to cut the trophy in half if I won. He laughed, and I pointed at the grinder.

As it turns out, Larry was voted the winner. No one was happier for him than me. He handled himself unlike a lot of the babies in this industry would have. Larry was there to have fun, and we started cutting away at the trophy. People were going absolutely nuts. I eventually walked off stage and joined the crowd. In my eyes, it was Larry's moment, and I didn't want to steal any of his thunder. They were throwing red-hot pieces of the trophy into the crowd, and people were diving for them with their bare hands. The crowd was literally in a frenzy, fighting for pieces of that trophy. I never could have imagined that that action would have received that kind of response. It was beautiful.

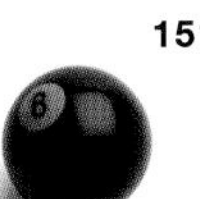

EPILOGUE

All I Want to Do is Build Bikes

154

ALL I really want to do is build custom bikes. That's not how we make our living now. We make our living off parts. I want to remain a part of the industry, but I want to build the bikes I want to build. We don't build the greatest bikes, but we have a sense of style.

Chopper Style

PEOPLE ASK me where chopper style is heading. I used to think it was turning toward the European style. Their style is very industrial. I think the Europeans were ahead of us, but now I think the Americans are moving ahead. Now I think things are moving more towards old school.

Sometimes at the end of a long day I'm too tired to ride home so I just sleep on a couch at the shop.

Someday I hope to have more time for things like hunting and fishing. *Author Photo*

People say the chopper craze will die out. I hope it's around 15 years from now. I have a lot of ideas that I want to make reality. I never quit thinking. Some of my thoughts are useless, sometimes it's just animosity coming out of me, and sometimes my thoughts are brilliant. A lot of times it's a combination of all of the above.

I think the future of choppers will involve a crossing of genres—not just crossing styles of bikes, but crossing different activities. The chopper of the future will have elements of hot-rod cars, elements of the surfing culture.

Time to wake up and do it all over again.

I've always liked to incorporate car parts into my choppers.

I'm building a hot rod–themed bike right now. My dad has always been into cars. One day he threw away a bunch of pistons and connecting rods, and I always wanted to use them in a chopper. The other day I got an idea to use a piston rod as a front downtube. It makes perfect sense. The rods are strong, forged steel and will make very functional downtubes.

I have a lot of other hot-rod ideas I want to use on the bike, too. I want to build an exhaust using a manifold from an old V-8. I might use a steering knuckle on a single-sided swingarm. I could use a car spindle with the disc brake and everything on it. It would be much cooler than any $5,000 single-sided swingarm I could buy off the shelf.

Car parts are cheap and they can look extremely cool on the right bike. I use a lot of cool parts I find on my bikes. I got a pile of shit in the back of the shop. I've got boxes marked "Billy's cool shit." I plan to use a lot of that on bikes some day.

The time is right for a bike like that. Everybody loves the bobber I just built. Five years ago they wouldn't have got it but now they get it.

As long as there's a breast that needs signing, I'll be there to sign it.

The Sincerest Form of Flattery?

THEY SAY THAT imitation is the sincerest form of flattery but I don't feel that way. When someone in the industry copies our style, I feel that's an insult. I appreciate being an inspiration—I had a lot of people inspire me when I started building bikes. My whole philosophy when I started was stay out of trouble, don't get some chick knocked up, don't let people be bad influences. I want to be an inspiration for kids. I want to show them how to make it. Someday I'd like to be a strong influence on someone, like Ron Finch and George Barris were to me.

In 15 years I'll be nearly 50 years old. I hope to still be building bikes, but I don't want it to be like it is now. I would like to have the time to find promising young builders and help them like other people helped me. Hell, I'd like to open up a chopper building school. And I'd like to have time to spend with my 11 wives, though I might have to move to Utah.

I get a lot of my ideas for building choppers from looking at cars.

What's Important?

PEOPLE come up to me all the time and say, "I'd love to have one of your bikes but I can't afford it." I say, "No, you can't buy one of my bikes because you decided to spend your money on other things. You decided to spend your money on your wife and two kids, on your $200,000 house, on your Yukon or Tahoe. If what you really wanted was one of my bikes, damn, Holmes, you fucked up."

I'm seeing a younger group of customers, guys who don't have wives and kids and all that other bullshit. They decided they're going to live in a shitty house, sell their Yukon, buy a cheap truck and spend their money on bikes.

On My Rails

WHEN I'M WORKING on a bike and everything comes together perfectly, when I see the vision I have in my head appearing in metal reality, I think to myself that I'm on my rails. It seems like that at those times my life is following the track it's supposed to follow, that I'm doing what I was meant to be doing.

Someday I'll probably settle down, but I don't see that happening any time soon.

The television stuff is great, but in the end for me it's still all about building cool choppers and riding them.

Even the strange twists and bends that have surprised me have led me to where I'm supposed to be. All the strange characters who've come into my life have been there for a reason. They've helped keep me on my rails.

I guess the reason for this is that I've pursued the things that give me the most satisfaction. The fire to build choppers would have burned me up if I had tried to do something else, if I had gotten on the track other people expected me to get on instead of following my own rails. Staying on my rails has brought me into contact with all the good people who have helped me get where I am today. My rails have led me into an industry where every day I get to do what I love to do.

Sometimes I work all night long, sleep a few hours on a couch at the shop, wake up and do it all over again. It's not because I have a deadline to meet or because I want to make even more money. It's because I love what I do. I love being on my rails.

☐ WARNING FOR

This warning is issued to you as a courtesy and to remind you to do your part in promoting safety on our highways and streets by closely following our traffic laws.

☑ EQUIPMENT REPAIR ORDER

You are requested to correct—immediately—the faulty or illegal equipment as indicated by the check marks below. Please return this ticket to this department within 5 days together with proper certification of inspection and approval.

NOTICE: If the indicated equipment is not repaired the vehicle shall not be operated.

☑ Headlamp	☐ Tail Lamp	☐ Reflectors
☐ Stop Lamp	☐ Clearance Lamp	☐ Turn Signal
☐ Brakes	☐ Defective Muffler	☐ Defective Horn
☐ Mirror	☐ Windshield Wiper	☐ Warning Devices

☐ Other __________

DRIVER'S SIGNATURE __________

OFFICER'S SIGNATURE __________

FLORIDA UNIFORM TRAFFIC CITATION 2997-CCD CHECK DIGIT X

COUNTY OF — ☐ (1) F.H.P. ☐ (2) P.D. ☑ (3) S.O. ☐ (4) OTHER

CITY (IF APPLICABLE) — AGENCY

IN THE COURT DESIGNATED BELOW THE UNDERSIGNED CERTIFIES THAT HE/SHE HAS JUST AND REASONABLE GROUNDS TO BELIEVE AND DOES BELIEVE THAT ON

SUMMONS (VIOLATOR'S COPY)

DAY OF WEEK — MONTH — DAY — YEAR — ☐ A.M. ☑ P.M.

NAME (PRINT) FIRST — MIDDLE — LAST

STREET — IF DIFFERENT THAN ONE ON DRIVER LICENSE "X" HERE

CITY — STATE — ZIP CODE

TELEPHONE NUMBER — DATE OF BIRTH MO — DAY — YR — RACE — SEX — HGT

DRIVER LICENSE NUMBER — STATE — CLASS — CDL LICENSE Y N — YR LICENSE EXP. — IF COMMERCIAL MTR. VEH. "X" HERE

YR. VEHICLE — MAKE — STYLE — COLOR — IF PLACARDED HAZARDOUS MATERIAL "X" HERE

VEHICLE LICENSE NO. — TRAILER TAG NO. — STATE — YEAR TAG EXPIRES — IF COMPANION CITATION(S) "X" HERE

UPON A PUBLIC STREET OR HIGHWAY, OR OTHER LOCATION, NAMELY

FT. — MILES — ☐ N ☐ S ☐ E ☐ W OF NODE

DID UNLAWFULLY COMMIT THE FOLLOWING OFFENSE. CHECK ONLY ONE OFFENSE EACH CITATION.

☐ UNLAWFUL SPEED ____ MPH SPEED APPLICABLE ____ MPH

(☐ INTERSTATE ☐ 4-LANE HWY WITH 20 FT. MEDIAN OUTSIDE BUS. OR RES. DIST.)

☐ CARELESS DRIVING	☐ SAFETY BELT VIOLATION	☐ EXPIRED DRIVER LICENSE
☐ VIOLATION OF TRAFFIC CONTROL DEVICE	☐ IMPROPER OR UNSAFE EQUIPMENT	☐ FOUR (4) MONTHS OR LESS
☐ VIOLATION OF RIGHT-OF-WAY	☐ EXPIRED TAG	☐ MORE THAN FOUR (4) MONTHS
☐ IMPROPER CHANGE OF LANE OR COURSE	☐ SIX (6) MONTHS OR LESS	☐ NO VALID DRIVER LICENSE
☐ IMPROPER PASSING	☑ MORE THAN SIX (6) MONTHS	☐ DRIVING WHILE LICENSE SUSPENDED OR REVOKED
☐ CHILD RESTRAINT	☐ NO PROOF OF INSURANCE	

☐ DRIVING UNDER THE INFLUENCE OF ALCOHOLIC BEVERAGES, CHEMICAL OR CONTROLLED SUBSTANCES, DRIVING/ACTUAL PHYSICAL CONTROL WHILE IMPAIRED, OR DRIVING/ACTUAL PHYSICAL CONTROL WITH UNLAWFUL BLOOD/URINE ALCOHOL LEVEL. BAL ____ %

OTHER VIOLATIONS OR COMMENTS PERTAINING TO OFFENSE:

☐ AGGRESSIVE DRIVING — IN VIOLATION OF STATE STATUTE — SECTION — SUB-SECTION

CRASH ☐ YES ☑ NO — PROPERTY DAMAGE ☐ YES $____ ☐ NO — INJURY TO ANOTHER ☐ YES ☐ NO — SERIOUS BODILY INJURY TO ANOTHER ☐ YES ☐ NO — FATAL ☐ YES ☐ NO

☐ CRIMINAL VIOLATION. COURT APPEARANCE REQUIRED, AS INDICATED BELOW.

☐ INFRACTION. COURT APPEARANCE REQUIRED, AS INDICATED BELOW.

☑ INFRACTION WHICH DOES NOT REQUIRE APPEARANCE IN COURT.

2997-CCD CHECK DIGIT X

COURT INFORMATION — DATE — TIME

COURT

LOCATION

PARKING FOR CHOPPERS ONLY

ALL OTHERS WILL BE VANDALIZED

FT. ____ MILES ____ ☐ N ☐ S ☐ E ☐ W OF NODE

DID UNLAWFULLY COMMIT THE FOLLOWING OFFENSE. CHECK ONLY ONE OFFENSE EACH TICKET.

☐ UNLAWFUL SPEED ____ MPH. SPEED APPLICABLE ____ MPH.

(☐ INTERSTATE ☐ 4-LANE HWY. WITH 20 FT. MEDIAN OUTSIDE BUS. OR RES. DIST.)

☐ CARELESS DRIVING	☐ SAFETY BELT VIOLATION	☐ EXPIRED DRIVER LICENSE
☐ VIOLATION OF TRAFFIC CONTROL DEVICE	☐ IMPROPER OR UNSAFE EQUIPMENT	☐ FOUR (4) MONTHS OR LESS
☐ VIOLATION OF RIGHT-OF-WAY	☐ EXPIRED TAG	☐ MORE THAN FOUR (4) MONTHS
☐ IMPROPER CHANGE OF LANE OR COURSE	☐ SIX (6) MONTHS OR LESS	☐ NO VALID DRIVER LICENSE
☐ IMPROPER PASSING	☐ MORE THAN SIX (6) MONTHS	☐ DRIVING WHILE LICENSE SUSPENDED OR REVOKED
☐ CHILD RESTRAINT	☐ NO PROOF OF INSURANCE	

☐ DRIVING UNDER THE INFLUENCE OF ALCOHOLIC BEVERAGES, CHEMICAL OR CONTROLLED SUBSTANCES; DRIVING/ACTUAL PHYSICAL CONTROL WHILE IMPAIRED, OR DRIVING/ACTUAL PHYSICAL CONTROL WITH UNLAWFUL BLOOD/URINE ALCOHOL LEVEL. BAL ____ %

OTHER VIOLATIONS OR COMMENTS PERTAINING TO OFFENSE:

IN VIOLATION OF: ☑ STATE STATUTE — SECTION — SUB-SECTION

CRASH ☑ YES ☐ NO — PROPERTY DAMAGE ☐ YES $____ ☐ NO — INJURY TO ANOTHER ☐ YES ☐ NO — SERIOUS BODILY INJURY TO ANOTHER ☐ YES ☐ NO — FATAL ☐ YES ☐ NO

☐ CRIMINAL VIOLATION. COURT APPEARANCE REQUIRED, AS INDICATED BELOW.

☐ INFRACTION. COURT APPEARANCE REQUIRED, AS INDICATED BELOW.

☐ INFRACTION WHICH DOES NOT REQUIRE APPEARANCE IN COURT.

253647-U CHECK DIGIT X

COURT INFORMATION — DATE — TIME

COLD HOT

You Have Violated

☐ Speeding
☐ Stop Sign
☐ Passing
☐ Following too Clos
☐ Fail to Yield
☐ Improper Turn
☐ Fail to Signal
☐ Drive on Wrong Si
☐ Fail to Dim
☐ Safety Belts/Child R
☐ Driver's License
☐ Registration
☐ Violation/Comment